SUCCESSFUL
projects

ISBN-13: 978-1732413900
ISBN-10: 1732413908

Published by:

Successful Projects Press
PO Box 1341
Dripping Springs, TX 78620
email: info@successfulprojects.com
www.successfulprojects.com

@2018 Successful Projects, LLC. All rights reserved.

Successful Projects, LLC content is copyright protected by U.S. intellectual property law that is recognized by most countries. To republish or reproduce Successful Projects' content, you must obtain our permission.

For pricing information or other inquiries, please contact Successful Projects Press.

Printed in the United States of America. No part of this work may be reproduced or transmitted in any form or by any means, electronic, manual, photocopying, recording, or by any information storage and retrieval system, without prior written permission of the publisher.

PMP and PMBOK are registered marks of the Project Management Institute, Inc.

Contents

Contents 1
Section 1: Introduction 1
    The Importance of Practice Exams 1
    Flow of this Workbook 1
Section 2: The PMP Credential Introduction 2
    Making a Project Out of Your Certification Goal 2
    My Plan for Reading the PMBOK® Guide 3
Section 3: PMBOK Framework and Foundations 4
    Project Definition 4
    Project Management Definition 4
    Organizational Structures 5
    Project Stakeholders 5
    Project Governance 6
    Project Life Cycles 6
    What is the difference between Standards and Regulations? 6
    Organizational Influences 6
    Distinguishing between EEFs and OPAs 8
Section 4: Knowledge Areas and Process Groups 9
    Understand the Basics First 9
    Process Names - Become Better Prepared by Practicing This 10
    Do These Steps to Fully Prepare 14
    Tips about ITTO's – Inputs, Tools & Techniques, and Outputs 16
    Project Management Knowledge Areas 16
        Integration Management (PMBOK Chapter 4) 16
        Scope Management (PMBOK Chapter 5) 17
        Schedule Management (PMBOK Chapter 6) 18
        Cost Management (PMBOK Chapter 7) 18

Quality Management (PMBOK Chapter 8) 19

Resource Management (PMBOK Chapter 9) 20

Communications Management (PMBOK Chapter 10) 20

Risk Management (PMBOK Chapter 11) 20

Procurement Management (PMBOK Chapter 12) 21

Stakeholder Management (PMBOK Chapter 13) 21

Section 5: Project Selection and Project Initiating Process Group 22

PROJECT SELECTION 22

Summary of the Project Selection Formulas 23

INITIATING PROCESS GROUP 25

4.1 Develop Project Charter 25

13.1 Identify Stakeholders 27

Section 6: Planning Processes – Integration and Scope 30

PLANNING PROCESS GROUP – INTEGRATION AND SCOPE 30

4.2 Develop Project Management Plan 30

5.1 Plan Scope Management 32

5.2 Collect Requirements 33

5.3 Define Scope 37

5.4 Create WBS 39

Section 7: Planning Processes – Schedule 43

PLANNING PROCESS GROUP - SCHEDULE 43

6.1 Plan Schedule Management 43

6.2 Define Activities 46

6.3 Sequence Activities 48

6.4 Estimate Activity Durations 50

6.5 Develop Schedule 54

Section 8: Planning Processes - Cost 64

PLANNING PROCESS GROUP - COST 64

7.1 Plan Cost Management 64

7.2 Estimate Costs 66

7.3 Determine Budget 67

Section 9: Planning Processes (continued) 69

PLANNING PROCESS GROUP – QUALITY, RESOURCE, COMMUNICATIONS, RISK, PROCUREMENT, and STAKEHOLDER ENGAGEMENT 69

8.1 Plan Quality Management 69

9.1 Plan Resource Management 75

9.2 Estimate Activity Resources 77

10.1 Plan Communications Management 78

11.1 Plan Risk Management 82

11.2 Identify Risks 84

11.3 Perform Qualitative Risk Analysis 86

11.4 Perform Quantitative Risk Analysis 87

11.5 Plan Risk Responses 89

12.1 Plan Procurement Management 91

13.2 Plan Stakeholder Engagement 94

Section 10: Executing Process Group 95

EXECUTING PROCESS GROUP 95

4.3 Direct and Manage Project Work 95

4.4 Manage Project Knowledge 96

8.2 Manage Quality 97

9.3 Acquire Resources 99

9.4 Develop Team 100

9.5 Manage Team 101

10.2 Manage Communications 103

11.6 Implement Risk Responses 106

12.2 Conduct Procurements 107

13.3 Manage Stakeholder Engagement 112

Section 11: Monitoring and Controlling Process Group 114

MONITORING AND CONTROLLING PROCESS GROUP 114

4.5 Monitor and Control Project Work 114

4.6 Perform Integrated Change Control 115

5.5 Validate Scope 116

5.6 Control Scope 117

6.6 Control Schedule 118

    7.4 Control Cost 123

    8.3 Control Quality 126

    9.6 Control Resources 128

    10.3 Monitor Communications 129

    11.7 Monitor Risks 130

    12.3 Control Procurements 131

    13.4 Monitor Stakeholder Engagement 132

Section 12: Closing Process Group 133

    CLOSING PROCESS GROUP 133

        4.7 Close Project or Phase 133

Section 13: Final Preparation for Your Exam 134

    Terminology Review 134

    Review Formulas and Other Cost and Financial Terminology 135

    The Week and Day before Your Exam 137

        One Week Before the Exam 137

    PMP Practice Exams 138

        Exam Tracking Log 138

        The Day Before the Exam 148

        At the Exam 148

        After the Exam 148

Answer Key 149

Section 3: PMBOK Framework and Foundations 149

    Project Definition 149

    Project Management Definition 149

    Organizational Structures 150

    Project Stakeholders 150

    Project Governance 151

    Project Life Cycles 151

    Difference between Standards and Regulations 151

    Organizational Influences 151

    Distinguishing between EEFs and OPAs 152

Section 4: Knowledge Areas and Process Groups 153

Understand the Basics First 153

Process Names 153

Project Management Knowledge Areas 154

    Integration Management (PMBOK Chapter 4) 154

    Scope Management (PMBOK Chapter 5) 154

    Schedule Management (PMBOK Chapter 6) 155

    Cost Management (PMBOK Chapter 7) 155

    Quality Management (PMBOK Chapter 8) 155

    Resource Management (PMBOK Chapter 9) 156

    Communications Management (PMBOK Chapter 10) 156

    Risk Management (PMBOK Chapter 11) 157

    Procurement Management (PMBOK Chapter 12) 157

    Stakeholder Management (PMBOK Chapter 13) 157

Section 5: Project Selection and Project Initiating Process Group 158

PROJECT SELECTION 158

INITIATING PROCESS GROUP 160

    4.1 Develop Project Charter ITTOs – PMBOK ® Guide Page 75 160

    13.1 Identify Stakeholders ITTOs – PMBOK ® Guide Page 507 161

Section 6: Planning Processes – Integration and Scope 163

Planning Process Group – Integration Management and Scope Management 163

    4.2 Develop Project Management Plan ITTOs – PMBOK ® Guide Page 82 163

    5.1 Plan Scope Management ITTOs – PMBOK ® Guide Page 134 163

    5.2 Collect Requirements – PMBOK ® Guide Page 138 164

    5.3 Define Scope – ITTOs PMBOK ® Guide Page 150 165

    5.4 Create WBS ITTOs – PMBOK ® Guide Page 156 166

Section 7: Planning Processes – Schedule 167

PLANNING PROCESS GROUP - SCHEDULE 167

    6.1 Plan Schedule Management ITTOs – PMBOK ® Guide Page 179 167

    6.2 Define Activities ITTOs – PMBOK ® Guide Page 183 167

    6.3 Sequence Activities ITTOs – PMBOK ® Guide Page 187 168

    6.4 Estimate Activity Durations ITTOs – PMBOK ® Guide Page 195 169

    6.5 Develop Schedule ITTOs – PMBOK ® Guide Page 205 171

Section 8: Planning Processes - Cost 176

PLANNING PROCESS GROUP – COST 176

7.1 Plan Cost Management PMBOK ® Guide Page 235 176

7.2 Estimate Costs - PMBOK ® Guide Page 240 176

7.3 Determine Budget – PMBOK ® Guide Page 248 177

Section 9: Planning Processes (continued) 178

PLANNING PROCESS GROUP – QUALITY, RESOURCE, COMMUNICATIONS, RISK, PROCUREMENT, and STAKEHOLDER 178

8.1 Plan Quality Management – PMBOK ® Guide Page 277 178

9.1 Plan Resource Management – PMBOK ® Guide Page 312 179

9.2 Estimate Activity Resources – PMBOK ® Guide Page 321 180

10.1 Plan Communications Management – PMBOK ® Guide Page 366 181

11.1 Plan Risk Management - PMBOK ® Guide Page 401 182

11.2 Identify Risks - PMBOK ® Guide Page 409 182

11.3 Perform Qualitative Risk Analysis - PMBOK ® Guide Page 419 183

11.4 Perform Quantitative Risk Analysis - PMBOK ® Guide Page 428 183

11.5 Plan Risk Responses - PMBOK ® Guide Page 437 184

12.1 Plan Procurement Management - PMBOK ® Guide Page 466 185

13.2 Plan Stakeholder Engagement - PMBOK ® Guide Page 516 186

Section 10: Executing Process Group 187

EXECUTING PROCESS GROUP 187

4.3 Direct and Manage Project Work - PMBOK ® Guide Page 90 187

4.4 Manage Project Knowledge - PMBOK ® Guide Page 98 187

8.2 Manage Quality - PMBOK ® Guide Page 288 187

9.3 Acquire Resources - PMBOK ® Guide Page 328 187

9.4 Develop Team - PMBOK ® Guide Page 336 187

9.5 Manage Team- PMBOK ® Guide Page 345 187

10.2 Manage Communications - PMBOK ® Guide Page 379 188

11.6 Implement Risk Responses - PMBOK ® Guide Page 449 189

12.2 Conduct Procurements - PMBOK ® Guide Page 482 189

13.3 Manage Stakeholder Engagement - PMBOK ® Guide Page 523 190

Section 11: Monitoring and Controlling Process Group 190

MONITORING AND CONTROLLING PROCESS GROUP 190

4.5 Monitor and Control Project Work - PMBOK ® Guide Page 105 190

4.6 Perform Integrated Change Control - PMBOK ® Guide Page 113 190

5.5 Validate Scope - PMBOK ® Guide Page 163 191

5.6 Control Scope - PMBOK ® Guide Page 167 191

6.6 Control Schedule - PMBOK ® Guide Page 222 191

7.4 Control Costs – PMBOK ® Guide Page 257 194

8.3 Control Quality Costs – PMBOK ® Guide Page 298 194

9.6 Control Resources Costs – PMBOK ® Guide Page 352 195

10.3 Monitor Communications – PMBOK ® Guide Page 388 195

11.7 Monitor Risks – PMBOK ® Guide Page 453 195

12.3 Control Procurements – PMBOK ® Guide Page 492 195

13.4 Monitor Stakeholder Engagement – PMBOK ® Guide Page 530 196

Section 12: Closing Process Group 197

CLOSING PROCESS GROUP 197

4.7 Close Project or Phase – PMBOK ® Guide Page 121 197

PMP® Exam Study Guide and Workbook

Section 1: Introduction

We wish to welcome you to a rewarding study program. The rewards include becoming a more knowledgeable project manager and becoming well-prepared to pass the Project Management Institute (PMI) Project Management Professional (PMP) certification exam. This workbook is written to accompany a workshop, college course, Successful Projects virtual class, instructor-led program or as a standalone resource. You will need a copy of the Project Management Institute's a Guide to the Project Management Body of Knowledge (PMBOK® Guide) – sixth edition, purchased separately, to complete the exercises.

The Importance of Practice Exams

Taking many practice exams is a very important part of your study process. But practice exams should not be your exclusive study method because all practice exams have questions that are different than what you will receive on your real exam. Yet, they still provide a pretty good indicator of how you might do on the real exam. They will also help provide you with an understanding of what topics you need to study further. Successful Projects has a full 200 question mock exam drawn from a much larger question bank available for purchase on our website.

Flow of this Workbook

This workbook's approach is to follow the order of the PMBOK® Guide – sixth edition processes in the flow that most project managers think of them, which is by the process groups as opposed to knowledge areas. We find project managers learn and retain this information better when they think of it this way. So, after we address the high-level topics, covered by the first three chapters of the PMBOK Guide, we then flow through processes in the order of initiating, planning, executing, monitoring & controlling, and closing. Each process starts with a review of the most important concepts, then it provides exercises to help you learn the harder skills, and it ends with the most challenging content that most project managers have to review prior to the exam.

After covering each of the processes, we address test preparation from a tactical standpoint, giving you a clear checklist of study work to do prior to sitting for and passing the exam.

Section 2: The PMP Credential Introduction

Making a Project Out of Your Certification Goal

We highly suggest that you treat your PMP® certification like a personal project. Make sure you have a good process planned. Create a WBS and schedule your time. Below you will find an example of a WBS for this.

1. Project: Getting my PMP Certification

    1.1. Confirm eligibility
    1.2. PMP Membership and Downloads
        1.2.1. Join PMI national
        1.2.2. Join local PMI chapter (optional)
        1.2.3. Download or purchase the latest PMBOK® Guide
    1.3. Initial Study Wave
        1.3.1. Read the PMBOK® Guide
            1.3.1.1. Read Chapters 1-3, and the intro of Chapter 4
            1.3.1.2. Read Chapter 5
            1.3.1.3. Read Chapter 6
            1.3.1.4. Read Chapter 7
            1.3.1.5. Read Chapter 8
            1.3.1.6. Read Chapter 9
            1.3.1.7. Read Chapter 10
            1.3.1.8. Read Chapter 11
            1.3.1.9. Read Chapter 12
            1.3.1.10. Read Chapter 13
            1.3.1.11. Read Chapter 4 (Out of order on purpose!)
            1.3.1.12. Read Part 2 – The Standard for Project Management and other Appendices
            1.3.1.13. Read the Glossary
        1.3.2. Obtain additional study materials (discuss with an instructor)
        1.3.3. Create a formula study sheet
    1.4. Create your PMP credential application with PMI
        1.4.1. Download the printable application (or find a template online)
        1.4.2. Document how you fit the eligibility requirements
        1.4.3. Collect proof of your educational requirements (35 hours completed)
        1.4.4. Project management work experience documentation
        1.4.5. List the projects you will include
        1.4.6. Use a Spreadsheet to document experience (create or find template online)
        1.4.7. List project information
        1.4.8. Contacts documentation
            1.4.8.1. Gather contact information
            1.4.8.2. Input the contact information
            1.4.8.3. Have contact review the application
        1.4.9. Submit the full application online
    1.5. Audit (if required)
    1.6. Milestone: Receive notice that PMI approves eligibility
    1.7. Send payment to PMI
    1.8. Intense study wave

      1.8.1. (Optional) Bootcamp, intense study group, or workshop
      1.8.2. Reread the PMBOK Guide
- 1.8.2.1. Read Chapters 1-3
- 1.8.2.2. Read Chapter 5
- 1.8.2.3. Read Chapter 6
- 1.8.2.4. Read Chapter 7
- 1.8.2.5. Read Chapter 8
- 1.8.2.6. Read Chapter 9
- 1.8.2.7. Read Chapter 10
- 1.8.2.8. Read Chapter 11
- 1.8.2.9. Read Chapter 12
- 1.8.2.10. Read Chapter 13
- 1.8.2.11. Read Chapter 4 (Out of order on purpose!)
- 1.8.2.12. Read Part 2 – The Standard for Project Management and all Appendices
- 1.8.2.13. Read the glossary

      1.8.3. Intense Practice Questions/Mock Exams
1.9. Schedule the exam
1.10. Take exam
- 1.10.1. Complete exam
- 1.10.2. Notify your family, friends, instructor, and coworkers
- 1.10.3. Celebrate

1.11. Recertification process begins the day you pass the exam
1.12. Plan how to earn 60 PDUs every 3 years
1.13. Earn your PDUs

My Plan for Reading the PMBOK® Guide

Plan how to fit study time into your schedule. Indicate a milestone schedule for the major work of this project (submit application, schedule test, finish reading the PMBOK Guide, take a full mock exam, etc.). Consider:

Will you keep notes or create flashcards as you read?

When will you schedule your reading?

What issues and interruptions should you plan for?

Section 3: PMBOK Framework and Foundations

Project Definition

A project is a **temporary** endeavor that is undertaken to create **unique** deliverables, products, services or results. It has a **definite beginning and an end**.

Project Characteristics

1. What would you say about the timeframe of a project?

2. What would you say about the project team?

3. It creates _____ or provides a solution.

4. It is "_____ of a kind" or unique.

5. It has specific measurable _____.

6. Allocated _____.

Project Management Definition

It is the application of knowledge, skills, tools, and techniques to project activities to meet project requirements.

Rewrite the definition of project management here in your own words:

Organizational Structures

There are three main types: Functional, Matrix (weak, balanced, and strong) and Project Oriented.

Remember that in the functional structure the project manager has the least authority and in the Project Oriented structure the project manager has the greatest authority.

In the Balanced Matrix the project manager and functional managers have equal levels of authority which may result in some conflicts created by the "two boss syndrome."

In the chart below, list what you feel might be the advantages and disadvantages of each type of organizational structure.

	Functional	Weak Matrix	Balanced Matrix	Strong Matrix	Project Oriented
Authority	PM has little to no authority	PM has low level of authority	PM has moderate or equal authority	PM has greater authority	PM has high level of authority
Advantages					
Disadvantages					

Project Stakeholders

Define the term and list examples:

Project Governance
Define the term in your own words and list examples:

Project Life Cycles

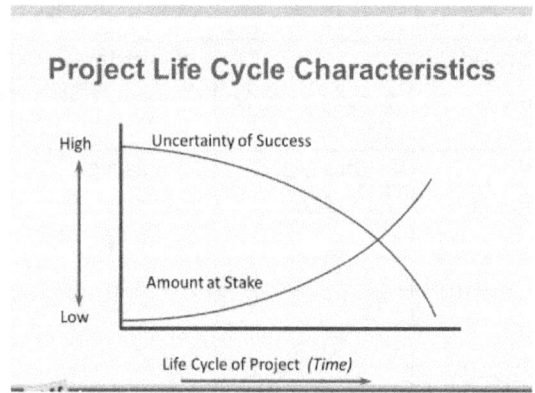

Study Note: Review the Generic Project Life Cycle Structure above. The amount at stake is low at the start, while risk is high. As the project progresses, the risk reduces and the amount at stake increases.

Development life cycles can be (name them):

1. P_____ 2. A_____ 3. It_____ 4. In____

_____ or 5. H_____.

What is the difference between Standards and Regulations?
See Glossary of the PMBOK Guide

Organizational Influences
Organizational Cultures and Styles: Note here how this impacts your management of projects:

Projects and Organizational Strategies - Consider the goals and objectives of your organization and how your project impacts or supports them. Make sure you can link your project to your organizational goals.

Project Management Information System – Note that this is ANY system or group of systems working together for use in gathering, storing, analyzing, and distributing project information. Examples include: Time Reporting Systems, Accounting Systems, Cost Management Systems, Project Software. These systems may be used to generate project status reports or information about the condition of the project such as variances and can be used to track the effect of approved changes. These are often software and database systems – but they can also be low-tech systems.

Work Authorization System - The processes that ensure the right work is done at the right time, in the right sequence.

Historical Records – Store information from previous projects and use that information when planning new projects. Learn from the lessons of past projects. Document lessons learned for use by others in the organization. Sharing lessons learned is also a factor in professional and social responsibility.

Enterprise Environmental Factors (EEFs)– Factors that may influence the planning process. Enterprise environmental factors are an input to many processes within the project management knowledge areas.

Note some influencing EEF examples from your projects here (or examples from 2.2 of PMBOK Guide):

Organizational Process Assets (OPAs)– These are the policies, procedures and processes that have been established within an organization. They will generally impact or in some way affect the planning of your projects.

Note some influencing OPA examples from your projects here (or examples from 2.3 of PMBOK Guide):

Distinguishing between EEFs and OPAs

Performing this exercise helps build a better understanding of the differences between two very commonly referenced inputs: The Enterprise Environmental Factors (EEFs – described in Section 2.2) and the Organizational Process Assets (OPAs – described in Section 2.3). Using the list below, circle if the item listed is an EEF or an OPA.

EEF	OPA	Stakeholder register templates
EEF	OPA	Organizational culture and structure
EEF	OPA	Lessons learned from previous projects or phases
EEF	OPA	Governmental or industry standards
EEF	OPA	Product standards
EEF	OPA	Stakeholder registers from previous projects
EEF	OPA	Global trends
EEF	OPA	Regional practices
EEF	OPA	Local habits
EEF	OPA	Political climate
EEF	OPA	Organizational communication requirements
EEF	OPA	Stakeholder notifications
EEF	OPA	Issue management procedures
EEF	OPA	Project reports
EEF	OPA	Project presentations
EEF	OPA	Organizational Risk Policy
EEF	OPA	Change Control procedures
EEF	OPA	Feedback from stakeholders

Section 4: Knowledge Areas and Process Groups

Understand the Basics First

There are 5 Process Groups and 10 Knowledge Areas. Review the 6th Edition PMBOK Guide page 25 and use that as a guide for completing these exercises.

How many total processes are in the PMBOK® Guide? _____

To begin your memory process, fill in the names of the 5 Process Groups and review page 25 of the PMBOK ® Guide to list and become familiar with the processes in each major process group:

Process Group Name	Total Processes Included
Total	

To remember the span of processes across the 10 knowledge areas, write the name of each knowledge area in the space provided and enter the number of processes in each:

(Study tip – all knowledge areas are integrated and interrelated.)

Knowledge Area	Total Processes Included
Total	

Process Names - Become Better Prepared by Practicing This

On the pages that follow you have a series of "fill-in-the -blank" matrix recreations based on p. 25 of the PMBOK. Most people can increase their familiarity and retention of the process names by hand writing each one of the 49 process names while thinking about what it is. Try to fill in as many as you can without looking at the answers. Then complete the grid by looking up what you could not remember. Let a little time pass, and then move on to the next page where you have less clues and repeat the same process.

You will not need to recreate the grid for the actual exam. However, many learners have told us that this exercise helps build the mental "scaffold" on which the rest of the PMBOK information is built. Envision that as you are performing your project management responsibilities, each of the 49 processes are constantly held in your subconscious mind. This exercise will help you do that.

Remembering the Process Names: Fill in 1 word

Think through the names of each process relative to their corresponding knowledge areas and process groups. Fill in the blanks. (Review page 25 in the PMBOK Guide frequently)

Knowledge Areas	Project Management Process Groups				
	Initiating Process Group	Planning Process Group	Executing Process Group	Monitoring & Controlling Process Group	Closing Process Group
Integration	4.1 Develop Project _____	4.2 Develop Project Management _____	4.3 Direct and Manage Project _____ 4.4 Manage Project _____	4.5 Monitor and Control Project _____ 4.6 Perform Integrated _____ _____	4.7 _____ Project or Phase
Scope		5.1 Plan _____ Management 5.2 Collect _____ 5.3 Define _____ 5.4 Create _____		5.5 _____ Scope 5.6 Control _____	
Schedule		6.1 _____ Schedule Management 6.2 Define _____ 6.3 _____ Activities 6.4 Estimate _____ Durations 6.5 Develop _____		6.6 Control _____	
Cost		7.1 Plan Cost _____ 7.2 _____ Costs 7.3 Determine _____		7.4 _____ Cost	
Quality		8.1 Plan _____ Management	8.2 _____ Quality	8.3 Control _____	
Resource		9.1 _____ Resource Management 9.2 Estimate Activity _____	9.3 _____ Resources 9.4 Develop _____ 9.5 _____ Team	9.6 Control _____	
Communications		10.1 Plan _____ Management	10.2 _____ Communications	10.3 Monitor _____	
Risk		11.1 Plan _____ Management 11.2 _____ Risks 11.3 Perform _____ Risk Analysis 11.4 Perform _____ Risk Analysis 11.5 Plan Risk _____	11.6 _____ Risk Responses	11.7 _____ Risks	
Procurement		12.1 Plan _____ Management	12.2 _____ Procurements	12.3 Control _____	
Stakeholder	13.1 _____ Stakeholders	13.2 _____ Stakeholder Engagement	13.3 Manage Stakeholder _____	13.4 _____ Stakeholder Engagement	

Remembering the Process Names: Fill in a few more words

Think through the names of each process relative to their corresponding knowledge areas and process groups. Fill in the blanks.

Knowledge Areas	Project Management Process Groups				
	Initiating Process Group	Planning Process Group	Executing Process Group	Monitoring & Controlling Process Group	Closing Process Group
Integration	4.1 _____ Project _____	4.2 _____ Project Management _____	4.3 _____ and Manage Project _____ 4.4 _____ Project _____	4.5 Monitor and _____ Project _____ 4.6 _____ Integrated _____ _____	4.7 _____ Project or_____
Scope		5.1 Plan _____ Management 5.2 Collect _____ 5.3 Define _____ 5.4 Create _____		5.5 _____ Scope 5.6 Control _____	
Schedule		6.1 _____ Schedule Management 6.2 Define _____ 6.3 _____ Activities 6.4 Estimate _____ Durations 6.5 Develop _____		6.6 Control _____	
Cost		7.1 Plan Cost _____ 7.2 _____ Costs 7.3 Determine _____		7.4 _____ Cost	
Quality		8.1 Plan _____ Management	8.2 _____ Quality	8.3 Control _____	
Resource		9.1 _____ Resource _____ 9.2 _____ Activity _____	9.3 _____ Team 9.4 Develop _____ 9.5 _____ Team	9.6 Control _____	
Communications		10.1 Plan _____ Management	10.2 _____ Communications	10.3 Monitor _____	
Risk		11.1 Plan _____ Management 11.2 _____ Risks 11.3 _____ _____ Risk Analysis 11.4 Perform _____ Risk Analysis 11.5 _____ Risk _____	11.6 _____ Risk _____	11.7 _____ Risks	
Procurement		12.1 Plan _____ Management	12.2 _____ Procurements	12.3 Control _____	
Stakeholder	13.1 _____ Stakeholders	13.2 _____ Stakeholder _____	13.3 _____ Stakeholder _____	13.4 _____ Stakeholder _____	

Remembering the Process Names: Fill in Process Groups, Knowledge Areas, and All Words by ID Numbers

Knowledge Areas	Project Management Process Groups				
	_____ Process Group	_____ Process Group	_____ Process Group	_____ Process Group	_____ Process Group
_____	4.1 _____	4.2 _____	4.3 _____ 4.4 _____	4.5 _____ 4.6 _____	4.7 _____
_____		5.1 _____ 5.2 _____ 5.3 _____ 5.4 _____		5.5 _____ 5.6 _____	
_____		6.1 _____ 6.2 _____ 6.3 _____ 6.4 _____ 6.5 _____		6.6 _____	
_____		7.1 _____ 7.2 _____ 7.3 _____		7.4 _____	
_____		8.1 _____	8.2 _____	8.3 _____	
_____		9.1 _____ 9.2 _____	9.3 _____ 9.4 _____ 9.5 _____	9.6 _____	
_____		10.1 _____	10.2 _____	10.3 _____	
_____		11.1 _____ 11.2 _____ 11.3 _____ 11.4 _____ 11.5 _____	11.6 _____	11.7 _____	
_____		12.1 _____	12.2 _____	12.3 _____	
_____	13.1 _____	13.2 _____	13.3 _____	13.4 _____	

Do These Steps to Fully Prepare

Here are some tips that might help you remember the processes better:

1. Note that the Planning and the Monitoring and Controlling (M&C) process groups are the only process groups that have a process for each of the ten knowledge areas.
2. Schedule Planning and Risk Planning both have five processes.
3. For Schedule Planning, those 5 processes flow quite logically from start to finish. Fill that part into your matrix first. Then bump over to put "Control Schedule" in its M&C process group, and you are done with the schedule processes. You may want to remind yourself that you are done with time, by putting an X through the remaining schedule process groups.
4. Remember that in the Monitoring & Controlling process group the very first process starts with both the actions to Monitor & Controlling Project Work. That is rather generic, and it helps when you think of it being the big-picture action of the Monitoring & Controlling process.
5. Realize that 8 out of the 12 processes in the Monitoring and Controlling Process Group have the word **control** in the process name. It is not always the first word – but it is in the name somewhere. Validate Scope and three areas that use the word "Monitor" are the exceptions. One technique to help you with this entire process group is to write Validate Scope into the Scope / M&C cell as the first thing and then write "Monitor" in the Communications, Risk and Stakeholder M&C cells.

Putting these building blocks into place helps retention. Once you have recreated the matrix 6 or 7 times, it will become routine and you find you will not have to think about these things very deeply. Going slow now (and considering all these points) will help you go fast and easily later!

Recreate the matrix of the 49 processes in the matrix of process groups and knowledge areas below:

Knowledge Areas	Project Management Process Groups					Process Count
Count:						

Tips about ITTO's – Inputs, Tools & Techniques, and Outputs

ITTOs are the Inputs, Tools and Techniques, and Outputs for the PMBOK Guide processes. Here are some helpful tips when trying to learn them.

1. Inputs and outputs are usually nouns or tangible items. Tools and techniques are usually verbs or some type of action.
2. A specific document, such as a WBS, will be shown as an output and listed the first time they are created as a document. Subsequently, project documents are updated frequently during the project life cycle and are shown as "project document updates" on the ITTO output list.
3. It is helpful to read the rules for handling ITTOs on p. 640 of the 6th Edition PMBOK.

Project Management Knowledge Areas

Integration Management (PMBOK Chapter 4)

1. In today's project environment what are some examples of balancing competing demands?

2. What are the 7 Integration processes?

    4.1 Develop _____ _____

    4.2 Develop _____ _____ _____

    4.3 Direct and _____ Project Work

    4.4 Manage _____ _____

    4.5 Monitor and _____ _____ _____

    4.6 Perform _____ _____ _____

    4.7 _____ _____ or Phase

Scope Management (PMBOK Chapter 5)

1. What are the 6 scope processes?

    5.1 Plan _____ _____

    5.2 Collect _____

    5.3 Define _____

    5.4 Create _____

    5.5 _____ _____

    5.6 Control _____

2. How does a WBS help a project team?

3. What is the difference between requirements and expectations?

    Requirements are _____

    Expectations are _____

    We differentiate between them because:

4. What is the scope baseline?

Schedule Management (PMBOK Chapter 6)

1. What is a project critical path?

2. What is fast tracking?

3. What is crashing?

4. What are the 6 schedule management processes?

   6.1 Plan _____ _____

   6.2 _____ _____

   6.3 Sequence _____

   6.4 Estimate _____ _____

   6.5 Develop _____

   6.6 Control _____

Cost Management (PMBOK Chapter 7)

1. What method of status reporting does the PMBOK promote for measuring cost variances?

2. What are the 4 cost management processes?

   7.1 _____ _____ _____

   7.2 Estimate _____

   7.3 Determine _____

   7.4 _____ _____

Quality Management (PMBOK Chapter 8)

1. What are the 3 quality processes?

   8.1 _____ _____ _____

   8.2 _____ _____

   8.3 _____ Quality

2. What are the words in the acronym PDCA cycle?
   P:

   D:

   C:

   A:

3. Page 274-275 of the PMBOK mentions key concepts for project quality management.
   1. Failure to meet quality requirements _____.
   2. Quality and _____ are not the same concepts.
   3. _____ over _____.
   4. Cost of _____.
   5. Five levels of increasingly effective quality management are:
      a. Most expensive approach is_____.
      b. _____ and _____ defects before sent to the customer.
      c. Use _____ to examine and correct the process.
      d. Incorporate _____ into the planning and designing of the product.
      e. Create a _____ that is committed to quality.

4. Do internet research on the definition of the Malcolm Baldrige Quality process and award. Get a high-level understanding of what types of organizations might care about this award.

5. Do internet research on the definition of ISO compatibility. What does ISO compatibility mean? "ISO" is derived from the Greek word "ISOS" meaning equal.

Resource Management (PMBOK Chapter 9)

1. What are the 6 resource management processes?

    9.1 _____ Resource Management

    9.2 _____ _____ _____

    9.3 Acquire _____

    9.4 Develop _____

    9.5 _____ Team

    9.6 _____ Resources

Communications Management (PMBOK Chapter 10)

1. What percent of their work time do most project managers spend communicating?

2. What are the 3 communication processes?

    10.1 _____ _____ _____

    10.2 _____ communications

    10.3 _____ communications

Risk Management (PMBOK Chapter 11)

1. What are the 7 risk processes?

    11.1 Plan risk _____

    11.2 _____ risks

    11.3 Perform _____ risk _____

    11.4 Perform _____ risk _____

    11.5 Plan risk _____

    11.6 _____ _____ Responses

    11.7 _____ Risks

2. What are the 5 positive risk responses?
    1. _____
    2. _____
    3. _____
    4. _____
    5. _____

3. What are the 5 negative risk responses?
    1. _____
    2. _____
    3. _____
    4. _____
    5. _____

Procurement Management (PMBOK Chapter 12)

1. Does procurement involve materials, services, or both?

2. What are the 3 procurement processes?

    12.1 _____ Procurement Management

    12.2 _____ Procurements

    12.3 _____ Procurements

Stakeholder Management (PMBOK Chapter 13)

1. What are the 4 stakeholder processes?

    13.1 _____ _____

    13.2 _____ Stakeholder _____

    13.3 _____ Stakeholder _____

    13.4 _____ Stakeholder _____

2. When does stakeholder identification start to occur?

Section 5: Project Selection and Project Initiating Process Group

In some cases, projects are initiated for compliance or regulatory reasons. A regulatory project may not yield positive financial results or improve overall organizational revenue generation but failure to complete them may have a legal and or a financial impact on the organization or may impact the ability to achieve strategic goals.

PROJECT SELECTION

Many organizational projects are selected based on financial indicators and anticipated market performance. Projects are generally assessed using some form of Economic Model. A general knowledge of each model is necessary as part of a project manager's business acumen.

Define these in your own words:

Time Value of Money _____

Opportunity Cost _____

Sunk Cost _____

Review these:

Payback Period – Time required to recover an initial investment.

Breakeven Analysis – Generally the point in time when cash flow out and cash flow in are equal.

Present Value (PV)– Also referred to as Discounted Cash Flow. It is the calculation that is used to determine the potential value of an investment by adjusting the future value (forecasted value) of the investment to the present value. Formula $PV = FV / (1+r)^n$.

Net Present Value – Used to determine the anticipated dollar value of an investment by summing up the present values for each year of the investment and then subtracting the initial investment. A project with a positive NPV is considered acceptable.

Internal Rate of Return – Determining the actual rate of return of an investment. This is an iterative process.

Depreciation – Determining the impact of the effects of time, wear, and the salvage value of capital investments.

Benefit / Cost ratio – Comparing the benefit of an investment with the cost of the investment. Generally, benefit should be greater than the cost of the investment for a project to be considered acceptable.

Summary of the Project Selection Formulas

Present Value	PV = FV / (1+r)^n
Future Value	FV = PV * (1+r)^n
Net Present Value	NPV = Select biggest number
Return on Investment	ROI = Select biggest number
Internal Rate of Return	IRR = Select biggest number
Payback Period	Add up the projected cash inflow minus expenses until you reach the initial investment. This is also referred to as the breakeven point.
Benefit to Cost Ratio	BCR = Benefit / Cost
Cost Benefit Ratio	CBR = Cost / Benefit
Opportunity cost	The value of the project not selected.

Net Present Value (NPV) Sample Problem

Your company is considering the purchase of new machinery to reduce operator costs. The cost to purchase the machine is $90k. Savings will start after 1 year. The cost impacts are projected to be:

Year	Savings	Factor	Present Value
0	-$90k		
1	$20k		
2	$40k		
3	$40k		
4	$40k		
5	$40k		

Assuming the cost of money is 10%, what would the NPV of this project be?

Payback Period Sample Problem:

A $50k investment is made and earns $35K/year. What is the payback period?

Benefit / Cost Ratio Sample Problem:

A $100k investment is made and earns $40K/year. What is the benefit/cost ratio after 5 years?

INITIATING PROCESS GROUP

4.1 Develop Project Charter

Understand the Basics First

Write the ITTO's for the process **Develop Project Charter** below:

Inputs	Tools & Techniques	Outputs
1.	1.	1.
2.	2.	2.
3.	3.	
4.	4.	

In the space below. For each ITTO, if the item listed is a generic category, list at least one example that could be included:

Make sure you understand the purpose of the project charter, which is to formally _____ the project or phase to begin and to begin committing _____.

Become Better Prepared by Practicing This

In the column on the left, fill in which input to the "Develop Project Charter" process is being described here. When you are done, check your answers in *PMBOK Guide pages 77-79*.

Which Input is referenced in the right column?	
	Project management procedures, safety policies, and a knowledge base.
	Includes things such as the organization's work authorization system.
	Documents that define the intent of the project and are usually legal in nature.
	Describes the need for the project and determines if the investment in the project is worthwhile.

Choose from these Inputs:

EEF

OPA

Agreements

Business Case

Do These Steps to Fully Prepare:

Indicate if these statements are true or false:

True or False: The project isn't a project until the charter is signed.

True or False: Writing the business case occurs outside the project boundaries.

True or False: Project management software is an EEF.

True or False: Political climate is an EEF.

True or False: If pressed to start a project before a signed charter is approved, a project manager should request the project charter gets approved prior to proceeding.

True or False: Lessons learned are an EEF.

13.1 Identify Stakeholders

Determine the people, organizations, suppliers, users and anyone who may be affected by the results of the project. Sometimes it will be obvious who the key stakeholders are, but for more complex projects, a formal analysis is likely to be helpful.

Understand the Basics First

Write the ITTO's for the process **Identify Stakeholders** below:

Inputs	Tools & Techniques	Outputs
1.	1.	1.
2.	2.	2.
3.	3.	3.
4.	4.	4.
5.	5.	
6.		
7.		

In the space below. For each ITTO, if the item listed is a generic category, list at least one example that could be included:

Stakeholders – A stakeholder is basically any person or organization either directly involved in or impacted by the project. Consider who the key stakeholders are for each project (sponsor, customer, project manager, end-user, supplier etc.) as well as other stakeholders who may view your project as a threat or an obstacle to their job position, project or organization (these are negative stakeholders). It is important to determine who the negative stakeholders are and what risks they may introduce during implementation and how they may interrupt the project or prevent the successful completion of your project. Use a data representation tool, such as a power/interest grid, to assist in developing strategies for managing different types of stakeholders. Create a stakeholder register to document your strategies.

Power/Interest Grid

It is important to understand some of the formal approaches project managers use in identifying and managing stakeholders. You can find many examples and variations of this approach on the Internet. In each quadrant, fill in the strategies that would generally be followed by a project manager when working with the stakeholders associated with each quadrant.

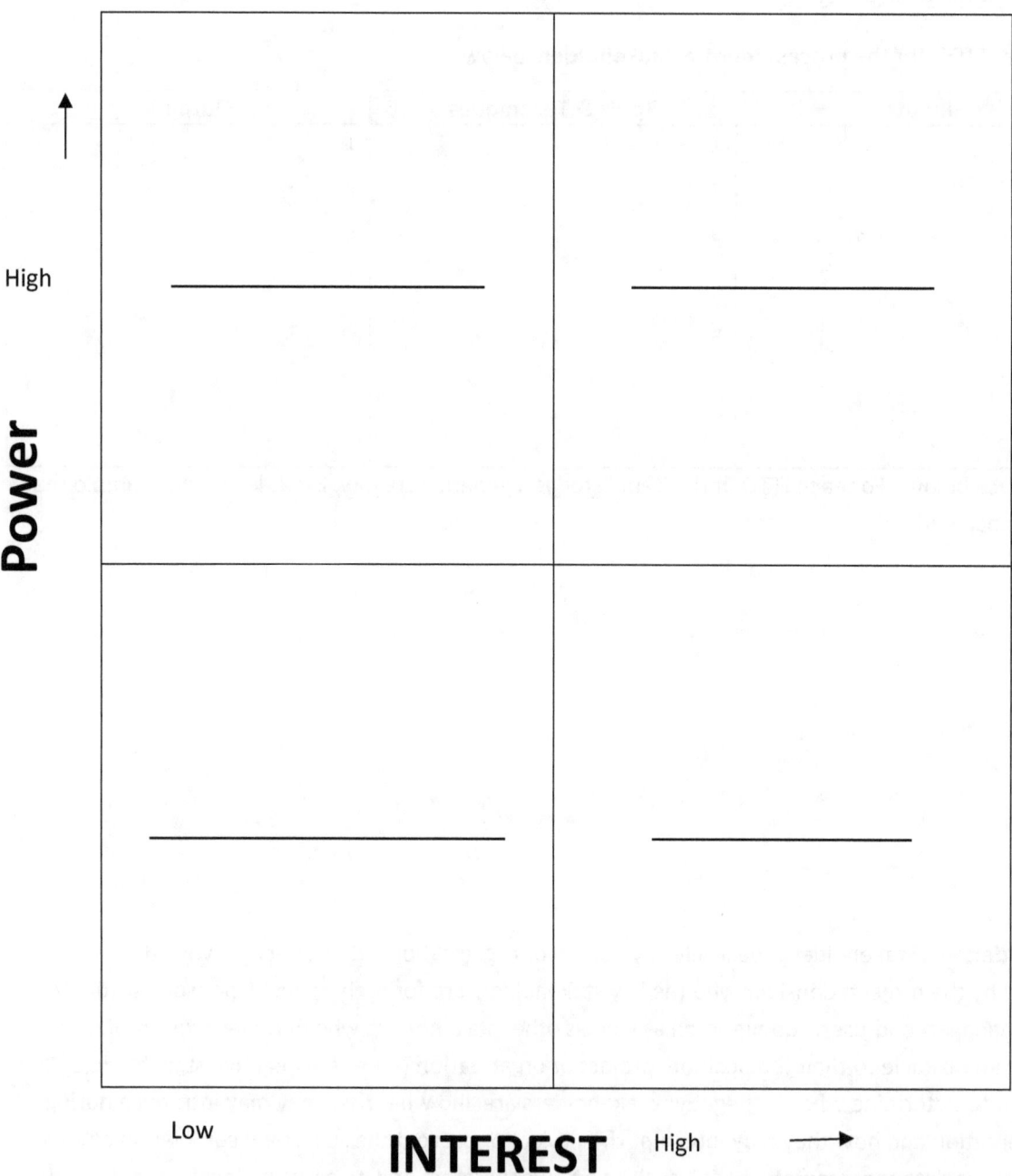

Perform These Steps to Fully Prepare

Salience Model

Fill in the three attributes that depict the relative importance of stakeholders as categorized by the Salience Model:

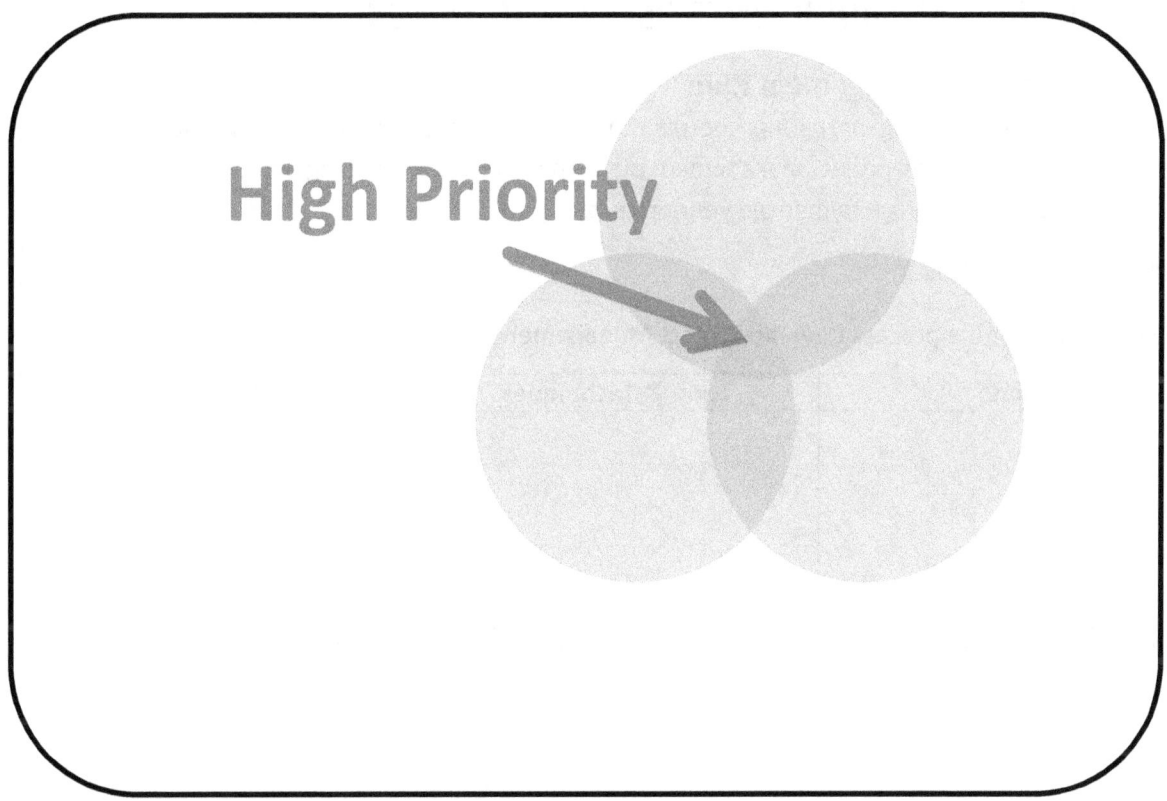

[See *PMBOK Guide* p. 513 for reference.]

Salience Model Stakeholder Types:
You can find examples of Salience Models on the Internet and in the Answer Key.

A.
B.
C.
D.
E.
F.
G.
H.

Section 6: Planning Processes – Integration and Scope

When your project has successfully obtained approval of your project charter and you have identified and analyzed the project stakeholders, you are ready to move into the planning processes. Planning is key to project success and the rigor of the project planning processes will aid you in creating an effective plan.

PLANNING PROCESS GROUP – INTEGRATION AND SCOPE

4.2 Develop Project Management Plan

This process involves defining, preparing, coordinating, and ultimately integrating all the subsidiary project plans into an overall project management plan. Think of this as defining and documenting the processes you are going to use to manage your project.

Understand the Basics First

Write the ITTO's for the process **Develop Project Management Plan** below:

Inputs	Tools & Techniques	Outputs
1.	1.	1.
2.	2.	
3.	3.	
4.	4.	

In the space below. For each ITTO, if the item listed is a generic category, list at least one example that could be included:

Subsidiary Plans - Detailed plans that support the overall project management plan. Subsidiary plans may include: Scope Change Control processes or plans, Schedule Change Control Plan, Cost Change Control plans, Resource management plan, Risk management plan, Safety plan, Cutover plan and other plans that may be necessary to support the project objectives and guide project execution.

Planning is a continuous process throughout the project life cycle. Projects are progressively elaborated (moving forward in increments, adding more detail in each step).

Become Better Prepared by Practicing This

Planning: What Goes in the Plan?

Project managers need to understand which documents to include in the project management plan. All of the documents listed below are commonly used. **Put a check next to those you would include in the project management plan.** When you are done, compare your answers to Table 4-1 on page 89 of the *PMBOK® Guide*.

- ☐ Work performance reports
- ☐ Project schedule network diagrams
- ☐ Stakeholder management plan
- ☐ Change requests
- ☐ Resource calendars
- ☐ Change management plan
- ☐ Activity list
- ☐ Quality control measurements
- ☐ Project staff assignments
- ☐ Communications management plan
- ☐ Schedule forecast
- ☐ Risk register
- ☐ WBS
- ☐ WBS dictionary
- ☐ Change log
- ☐ Project scope statement
- ☐ Configuration management plan
- ☐ Requirements traceability matrix
- ☐ Resource management plan
- ☐ Activity resource requirements
- ☐ Agreements
- ☐ Basis of estimates
- ☐ Quality checklists
- ☐ Project statement of work
- ☐ Cost baseline
- ☐ Scope management plan
- ☐ Work performance data
- ☐ Team performance assessments
- ☐ Project calendars
- ☐ Process improvement plan
- ☐ Activity attributes
- ☐ Seller proposals
- ☐ Schedule baseline
- ☐ Cost management plan
- ☐ Cost forecast
- ☐ Activity cost estimates
- ☐ Procurement management plan
- ☐ Schedule data
- ☐ Schedule management plan
- ☐ Requirements management plan
- ☐ Resource breakdown structure
- ☐ Quality metrics
- ☐ Risk management plan
- ☐ Milestone list
- ☐ Issue log
- ☐ Source selection criteria
- ☐ Procurement documents
- ☐ Procurement statement of work
- ☐ Project charter
- ☐ Stakeholder register
- ☐ Project funding requirements
- ☐ Project schedule
- ☐ Requirements documentation
- ☐ Work performance information
- ☐ Activity duration estimates
- ☐ Quality management plan

Do These Steps to Fully Prepare

Understanding Baseline Plans
(Complete this sentence)

Once the project management plan is baselined, it may only be changed when….

5.1 Plan Scope Management
This defines the processes you have selected to use to help define, validate, and control the project's scope. This is about guidance and direction of your management processes.

Understand the Basics First

Write the ITTO's for the process **Plan Scope Management** below:

Inputs	Tools & Techniques	Outputs
1.	1.	1.
2.	2.	2.
3.	3.	
4.		

In the space below. For each ITTO, if the item listed is a generic category, list at least one example that could be included:

Become Better Prepared by Practicing This

Pay special attention to the two outputs from Plan Scope Management. List and describe what they are again here:

1. _____

2. _____

Do These Steps to Fully Prepare

Do you fully understand what configuration management and a configuration management system is?

This may be part of a requirements management plan and other parts of project planning. If you don't understand what this is, review the definition in the glossary and research examples of this on the internet.

5.2 Collect Requirements

The process of Collect Requirements refers to the processes of gathering high level requirements from stakeholders and, as the project is progressively elaborated, the specific functional requirements of a product or service as defined by the end-users or other stakeholders. Collect requirements assists in developing a more complete understanding of the scope of the project.

Understand the Basics First

Collect Requirements - Defining and documenting the needs of the project stakeholders. Project requirements include resources, materials, and equipment necessary to produce project deliverables. Product requirements are associated with functionality, features, and physical characteristics. The project charter may include high level descriptions of requirements that will be elaborated as the project plan is developed.

The statement "I want this application to have password protection." is a technical specification, not a requirement. The requirement is "it must be secure from unauthorized access."

Write the ITTO's for the process **5.2 Collect Requirements** below:

Inputs	Tools & Techniques	Outputs
1.	1.	1.
2.	2.	2.
3.	3.	
4.	4.	
5.	5.	
6.	6.	
7.	7.	
	8.	

In the space below. For each ITTO, if the item listed is a generic category, list at least one example that could be included:

Data Gathering Techniques - Project teams may use a variety of techniques to gather information and determine product requirements. List and describe them here and reference PMBOK® Guide 5.2.2 Collect Requirements: Tools and Techniques if you need help.

Become Better Prepared by Practicing This

Study the *PMBOK Guide* Figure 5-5 Collect Requirements Data Flow Diagram.

Pay special attention to the bold dotted lines.

- Imagine what problems you might experience if you were trying to control the project's scope before you had your requirements documented.

- What issues might arise from creating your WBS prior to collecting requirements?

- What problems would you have if you collected your requirements prior to having a scope management plan?

Validate that you understand the difference between these methods for making decisions. Write a brief description on how the listed approach would be used to make a decision on a requirement dispute.

Unanimity: _____

Majority: _____

Plurality: _____

Autocratic: _____

Check your answers against 5.2.2.4 Decision Making in the *PMBOK® Guide*.

Plurality is the term that many people have difficulty remembering because it is not as commonly used as the other terms. Consider putting the definition of plurality on a flash card.

Do These Steps to Fully Prepare

Requirements traceability matrix - A Requirements Traceability Matrix is a tabular format that provides the ability to follow and audit the life of a requirement. In both a forward and backward direction, from its origins through its realization in the design and functional specifications, to its eventual development.

The specifics of a Requirements Traceability Matrix will vary depending upon your industry, project complexity, and organizational requirements. However, it is important that you have a clear vision of this project document in your mind. **Use the space below to sketch a grid form/template that contains headers for the type of requirements traceability matrix that you might use.** After you have imagined and sketched this grid below, check with the example found on p. 149 in the *PMBOK® Guide* and reread section 5.2.3.2 if you need further clarification about the use and attributes of the traceability matrix.

(Space left blank for exercise above.)

5.3 Define Scope

The Define Scope process produces the **Project Scope Statement**. The scope statement provides detailed information about the project and answers the "What? Who? How? Why? When? Where?" questions that will clarify the purpose of the project and what work must be completed by the project team.

Understand the Basics First

Remember that Enterprise Environmental factors and Organizational process assets are common inputs to many process groups. Examples of enterprise environmental factors include: organizational culture, infrastructure, human resources, and risk tolerance. Organizational process assets include policies and procedures such as change control and centralized purchasing.

Write the ITTO's for the process **Define Scope** below:

Inputs	Tools & Techniques	Outputs
1.	1.	1.
2.	2.	2.
3.	3.	
4.	4.	
5.	5.	

In the space below. For each ITTO, if the item listed is a generic category, list at least one example that could be included:

Become Better Prepared by Practicing This

What is the difference between a Project Charter and a Scope Statement?

Do These Steps to Fully Prepare

The Project Scope Statement answers the questions: What are we doing? Why? Who will do the work? When is it needed? Where will the work be done? How will the work be done? Refer to page 154, *PMBOK® Guide* for additional information about the Scope Statement.

If you have not seen professional project scope statements, search the Internet to see examples. Analyze them against what the *PMBOK® Guide* recommends for Scope Statements.

Note examples of constraints on your projects:

Note examples of assumptions on your projects:

Define Scope Outputs:

The project scope statement will be developed, and project documents previously developed will be updated to reflect any changes or newly obtained project related information.

5.4 Create WBS

Subdivide the project into smaller more manageable parts through the process of decomposition.

Understand the Basics First

Write the ITTO's for the process **Create WBS** below:

Inputs	Tools & Techniques	Outputs
1.	1.	1.
2.	2.	2.
3.		
4.		

In the space below. For each ITTO, if the item listed is a generic category, list at least one example that could be included:

Create WBS –The WBS is created using the process of **decomposition** (breaking down large items into smaller more manageable elements). WBS templates will accelerate the process and may be developed by using previous projects. A PMO may develop standard WBS templates for use during project planning.

The WBS breaks the project down into smaller more manageable components and allows for more effective and reliable time and cost estimating. WBS development produces a hierarchical grouping of project components and tasks and *is not intended to display the sequence of tasks and activities.*

What are the benefits associated with developing and using a Work Breakdown Structure?

A WBS dictionary provides more detailed information about WBS components. Here is an example:

WBS Dictionary (Task Description)			
Project Name	Job and Task No	Date Issued	Person Assigned
Length	Due Date	Budget	Sign Off/Approver

Task Description
Goals and objectives
Product description
Acceptance criteria
Interdependencies: Before this task _____ After this task _____
Contact for any questions or concerns:

The Scope baseline is produced in the Create WBS process and is defined as the WBS, Scope statement, and all approved changes.

The WBS is referred to as the "cornerstone of all planning" and it is usually constructed using phases or major deliverables, depending on the project manager's preference. The WBS is developed using the 100% rule – the elements in one level should equal 100% of the higher or parent level.

Other views and breakdown structures to remember:

RBS: Resource breakdown structure. Sorted by work package assignments or owners.

OBS: Organizational breakdown structure. Sorted by performing organizational departments or units.

The Scope baseline includes (complete this in your own words):

Become Better Prepared by Practicing This

Understand the Terms Code of Accounts and Control Accounts

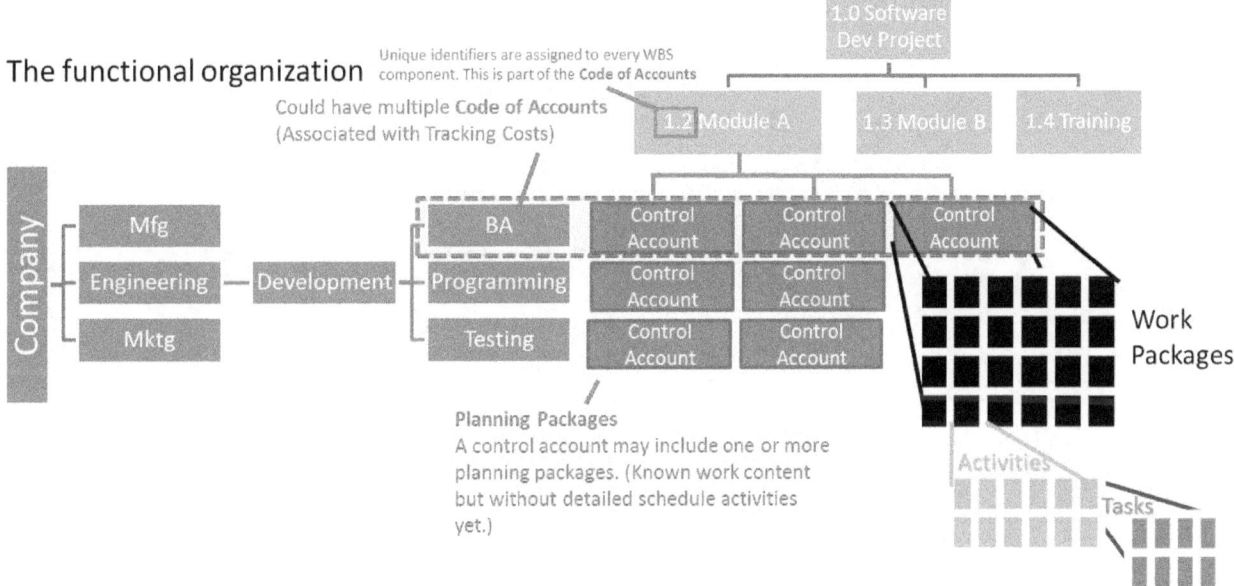

Reread about Work Package in 5.4.3.1 of the *PMBOK® Guide*. Make sure you understand what the "Code of Accounts" and a "Control Account" are used for. Write the definition of each.

Code of Accounts: _____

Control Account: _____

Do These Steps to Fully Prepare

Practice developing and using the WBS. If you do not have extensive exposure to WBSs, do an Internet search to view many sample project WBS examples. Use the space below to practice.

Section 7: Planning Processes – Schedule

PLANNING PROCESS GROUP - SCHEDULE

6.1 Plan Schedule Management

Understand the Basics First

Write the ITTO's for the process **Plan Schedule Management** below:

Inputs	Tools & Techniques	Outputs
1.	1.	1.
2.	2.	
3.	3.	
4.		

In the space below. For each ITTO, if the item listed is a generic category, list at least one example that could be included:

Become Better Prepared by Practicing This

Considerations for Agile/Adaptive Environments

"Adaptive approaches use short cycles to undertake work, review the results and adapt as necessary." Does this adaptive environment change the role of the project manager?

Rolling Wave Planning – An iterative Planning Technique in which the work to be accomplished in the near term is planned in detail while the work in the future is planned at higher level. It is the process of project planning in waves as the project proceeds and later details become clearer; similar to the techniques used in agile software development approaches such as Scrum.

PDM – Precedence Diagramming Method. This method has 4 logical relationships: FS – finish to start, FF – finish to finish, SF- start to finish, SS – start to start. The most common relationship is FS.

Lag – Delayed time. This is not float. Lag is associated with a specific requirement to wait for a defined period of time before beginning the next succeeding task. Lag can be a factor when calculating the critical path.

Lead – Accelerates the project schedule. Succeeding tasks are initiated before the completion of their predecessors, similar to fast tracking.

CPM – Critical path method. This determines early start and finish and late start and finish for each activity.

Milestone – Significant point in time. Does not have a duration and does not consume resources.

Slack – Also known as float. It basically means flexibility. The amount of time an activity can slip without affecting the project end date. There is generally no float or slack on the critical path.

Critical Path – This is the longest path through the network that determines the earliest completion date of the project. Critical path method. This determines early start and finish and late start and finish for each activity.

Forward pass – Determines early start and finish dates. Remember to use the larger number at points of convergence. The forward path begins at the start of the project and follows each path through the project to the end milestone.

Backward pass – Determines late start and finish dates. Use the lowest number at points of convergence. The backward pass begins at the end of the project and follows all paths back to the start milestone.

Float – The amount of time an activity can slip in time before affecting the project end date.

Free Float – The amount of time an activity can slip before affecting its immediate successor activities.

PERT – The weighted average formula is: (Optimistic + 4 Most Likely + Pessimistic) / 6

Do These Steps to Fully Prepare

The Output - Schedule Management Plan

Can establish, among other things:

Schedule Model Development – The scheduling methodology and tool to be used.

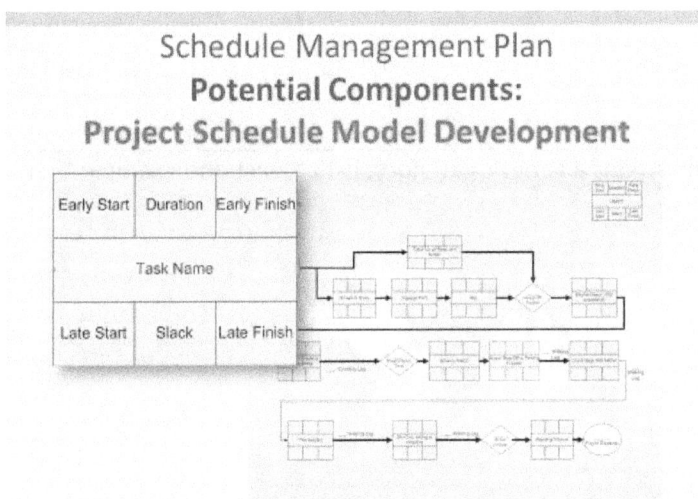

Levels of Accuracy - Example

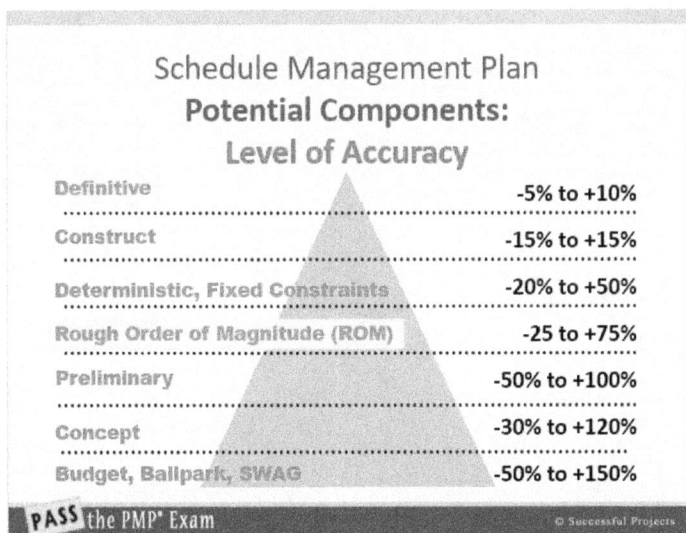

What are levels of accuracy and how would they be determined and used?

6.2 Define Activities

Underline: Understand the Basics First

Write the ITTO's for the process **Define Activities** below:

Inputs	Tools & Techniques	Outputs
1.	1.	1.
2.	2.	2.
3.	3.	3.
	4.	4.
		5.

In the space below. For each ITTO, if the item listed is a generic category, list at least one example that could be included:

Become Better Prepared by Practicing This

Define Work Packages and Activities

Define Rolling Wave Planning

How do you know when your WBS has been decomposed to the right level?

What is the difference between work activities and milestones?

LOE is an acronym for _____

Define LOE in your own words:

Do These Steps to Fully Prepare

Activity Attributes

Fill in the blanks below from section 6.2.3.2 Activity Attributes on page 186 in the *PMBOK® Guide*.

Activity attributes extend the description of the activity by identifying the multiple components associated with each activity. The components for each activity evolve over time. During the initial stages of the project, they include the _____, _____, and _____. When completed, they may include _____, _____, _____, _____, _____ (Section 6.3.2.3), _____, _____, _____, and _____. Activity attributes can be used to identify the _____ where the work has to be performed, the project _____ the _____ is assigned to, and _____ involved. Activity attributes are used for schedule development and for selecting, ordering, and sorting the planned schedule activities in various ways within reports.

6.3 Sequence Activities

Understand the Basics First

Write the ITTO's for the process **Sequence Activities** below:

Inputs	Tools & Techniques	Outputs
1.	1.	1.
2.	2.	2.
3.	3.	
4.	4.	

In the space below. For each ITTO, if the item listed is a generic category, list at least one example that could be included:

Become Better at Practicing This

Remember the four dependency types? Mandatory (hard logic), Discretionary (Soft logic), External dependencies (dependencies that are outside of the actual project, the team has no control over, and can affect the project critical path) and Internal dependencies (generally inside the teams control).

Give brief examples of each type

Common Types of Dependency Relationships

Activity sequencing produces the project network diagram. The network diagram shows predecessor / successor relationships, (the logical relationships between activities). The precedence diagramming method (PDM) is used to create a network diagram. The PDM uses four types of logical relationships.

Listed from most to least common

Finish-to-Start: The task to the left must be completed before the task to the right can start. This is by far the most commonly used dependency relationship in network diagrams, accounting for over 90% of most dependency relationships.

Finish-to-Finish: The second task cannot finish until the first task finishes. For example, "Inspect Electrical" cannot finish until "Add wiring" finishes.

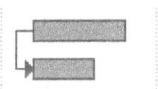

Start-to-Start: The second task cannot start until the first task starts. For example, if you "Pour foundation" first, you can and should begin the process to "Level Concrete".

Start-to-Finish: The second task cannot finish until the first task starts. For example, a new accounts payable system has to start before the old accounts payable system can be shut down. Note: the SF relationship is rarely used.

Lead and Lag

Lead means accelerate – start an activity before its predecessor is complete.

Lag is a delay in time. An activity cannot start for a period time after its predecessor has been completed. Example – Pour concrete, then wait for it to cure before removing the forms.

Become Better Prepared by Practicing This

Define these terms in your own words:

Hammock Activity

Hanger

Do These Steps to Fully Prepare

Is this lead or lag?

Scheduling dependencies	Lead or Lag?
1. You want to plan to utilize PMP practice questions one week after you have started reading your *PMBOK Guide*.	
2. The hardcopy of the *PMBOK Guide* that you ordered online will require 3 days of delivery time prior to when you can start reading it.	
3. The room you have painted needs one day of drying time before you can hang curtains.	
4. You determine you should start putting out food 30 minutes prior to the scheduled arrival of your guests.	
5. You need the outgoing team member to train the incoming team member for 1 week prior to the outgoing team member is leaving	

6.4 Estimate Activity Durations

Write the ITTO's for the process **Estimate Activity Durations** below:

Understand the Basics First

Inputs	Tools & Techniques	Outputs
1.	1.	1.
2.	2.	2.
3.	3.	3.
4.	4.	
	5.	
	6.	
	7.	
	8.	

In the space below. For each ITTO, if the item listed is a generic category, list at least one example that could be included:

Define Best Practices (In your own words)

The process of **Estimate Activity Durations** is related to time estimating and it starts by determining resource capabilities, reviewing historical information, and the use of analogous estimates, reserve time, contingencies, calendars, and three-point estimates (optimistic, most likely, and pessimistic estimates).

PERT Formula or Weighted Average Estimate – A type of three point estimating calculation in which the Optimistic value is added to 4 times the most likely value plus the pessimistic value and then dividing that result by 6 to obtain a weighted average estimate. The weighted formula is expressed as:

{Optimistic + 4(most likely) + pessimistic} / 6

Know the Types of Estimating Approaches – **Analogous and Parametric Estimating** (page 200-201 PMBOK Guide)

Consider the application of each type of estimate and the reliability of the estimating process. Cost Estimating may involve the use of Analogous, Parametric, and Bottom up estimates.

Top-Down Estimates

1. _____ estimates use previous similar projects as a basis for estimating.
2. _____ estimates use a mathematical model such as total square feet multiplied by the cost per square foot.

Bottom-Up Estimates

Bottom-up estimates are also known as engineering or grass roots estimates and the WBS is utilized in the process to create a "definitive estimate". A bottom-up estimate will generally produce an estimate that is within + or – 10% of the actual result. The bottom-up estimate requires the greatest effort, in terms of time and resources, to produce.

Become Better Prepared by Practicing This

Sigma Exercise #1

Fill in the % of confidence or the probabilities in a normal distribution curve as follows:

1 sigma = _____ confidence level. This is within + or minus one standard deviation from the mean.

2 sigma = _____ confidence level. This is within + or minus two standard deviations from the mean.

3 sigma = _____ confidence level. This is within + or minus three standard deviations from the mean.

6 sigma = _____ confidence level. This is within + or minus six standard deviations from the mean.

Do These Steps to Fully Prepare

Weighted PERT Practice Exercises

Optimistic: 2　Most Likely: 4　Pessimistic: 6	Optimistic: 10　Most Likely: 20　Pessimistic: 30	Optimistic: 25　Most Likely: 50　Pessimistic: 83
What is the expected duration?	What is the expected duration?	What is the expected duration?

List approaches to Group Decision Making:

What is Reserve Analysis?

Practice using the Probability Associated with Normal Distribution Curve

Remember that there is a 68.5 % probability within 1 standard deviation from the mean, 95 % probability within 2 standard deviations from the mean, 99.73% within 3 standard deviations from the mean.

Practice this with the question below (without looking at the answer if you can).

Question:

An Example of a Compound Question

As the project manager for the Fusion Energy Project you have developed the following schedule information for project completion: Optimistic = 10 weeks, Pessimistic = 30 weeks and most likely time = 20 weeks. Using the weighted average technique you determine that there is a 95% probability that the project duration will be what?

A. Between 16.7 and 23.33 weeks
B. Between 20.0 and 23.33 weeks
C. Between 13.4 and 26.66 weeks
D. Between 16.7 and 26.22 weeks

6.5 Develop Schedule

Determining the planned start and finish dates for all project activities.

<u>Understand the Basics First</u>

Write the ITTO's for the process **Develop Schedule** below:

Inputs	Tools & Techniques	Outputs
1.	1.	1.
2.	2.	2.
3.	3.	3.
4.	4.	4.
5.	5.	5.
	6.	6.
	7.	7.
	8.	

In the space below. For each ITTO, if the item listed is a generic category, list at least one example that could be included:

Note examples of these factors in your projects:

Resource Calendars _____

Constraints _____

Develop Schedule: Consider availability, capability, number of resources needed, the work calendar, skill levels, vacations, sick time, external issues such as weather, lead or lag requirements, resource leveling, schedule compression (fast tracking and crashing), what-if scenarios, and Critical Path Method (CPM).

Become Better Prepared by Practicing This

Network Diagramming – Calculation Instructions

1. Flow chart the activities in the order that the work needs to be done.

    a. Put the Task Names or IDs in the boxes and draw dependencies with arrows
    b. Insert the Duration Estimate for each box. You may use any time units (such as hours, days, weeks, months, or years) but remember to be consistent by using the same unit of measurement throughout the project. The most common choice is business days.

2. Calculate the forward pass to determine the early start and finish for the work.

    a. Put 1 in the Early Start for the work that can begin at the start.
    b. Add the Early Start number to the Duration number. Then subtract one. That becomes the Early Finish number of the first task.
    c. Add one to the Early Finish from that task and put it into the Early Start of the tasks coming off that box.
    d. When faced with a sink point (aka convergent point), the Early Start that we use is the largest of the Early Finish numbers from the preceding boxes.

3. Calculate the backward pass from right to left. This fills in the Late Start and Late Finish for each task. Below are step-by-step instructions for helping to do that:

    a. Begin the backward pass at the end of the project. Take the number in the Early Finish of the Last Task, or in the end marker, and put it into the Late Finish of the same task.
    b. From the Late Finish, subtract the task duration and add one to get the number for the Late Start. Remember you are working from right to left now.
    c. As you move left in the tasks, subtract one from the late start task to fill in the late finish of connected tasks.
    d. When you have multiple choices, the Late Start that carries to the predecessors Late Finish is the smallest number of the options.
    e. Calculate the Slack/Float for each task. The value of the Slack/Float is calculated as the difference between the Early Start and the Late Start.

4. Find the critical path and mark it in red. The critical path is the longest path through the project schedule. All of the activities on that path will have 0 slack.
5. Calculate the calendar dates that correspond with the schedule numbers, depending upon when you plan to start the first tasks.
6. Perform workload leveling (which lengthens the schedule)

    a. Bypass any non-work days.
    b. Communicate with the team members regarding schedule and accommodate the project schedule for conflicts.

Common Types of Imposed Dates (Constraints)

- **Fixed Early Start**: A tasks early state date is set to the imposed date. It does not affect the tasks late date calculations.
- **Fixed Early Finish**: A tasks early finish is set to the imposed date. It does not affect the tasks late date calculations.
- **Fixed Late Start**: A tasks late start is set to the imposed date. It does not affect the tasks early date calculations.
- **Fixed Late Finish**: A task must finish on the imposed date. It does not affect the early date calculations.
- **Start Not Earlier Than**: A task cannot finish earlier than the imposed date. This has implications on late start-finish dates.
- **Start Not Later Than**: A task cannot start later than the imposed date. This has implications on early start-finish dates.
- **Finish Not Later Than**: A task cannot finish later than the imposed date. This has implications on early start-finish dates with the potential for float.
- **Must Start On**: Customer or organization-imposed start date; driven by project start.
- **Must Finish On**: Customer or organization-imposed finish date; potential for negative float.
- **Work Between**: Must work between two imposed dates; potential for negative float.

Network Calculation Exercises

Do these exercises one at a time. Start with the forward pass to the end of the project. Then calculate the backward pass. Finally, mark the critical path. Check your answers in the answer key.

Early Start	Duration	Early Finish
Task Name or ID		
Late Start	Slack	Late Finish

Very Easy

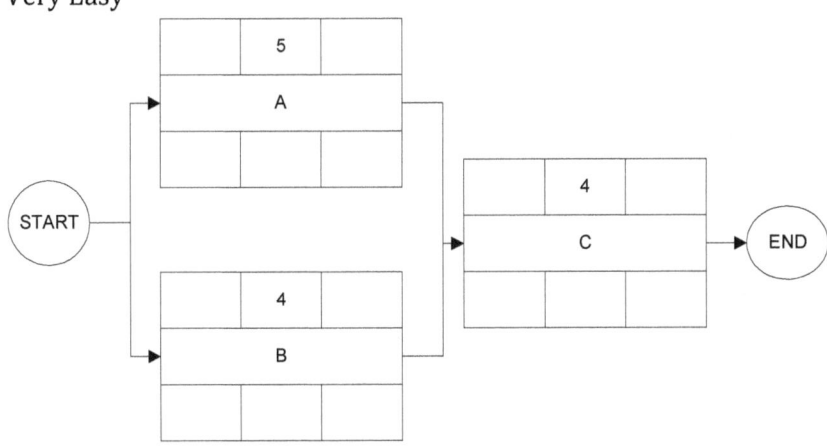

Easy

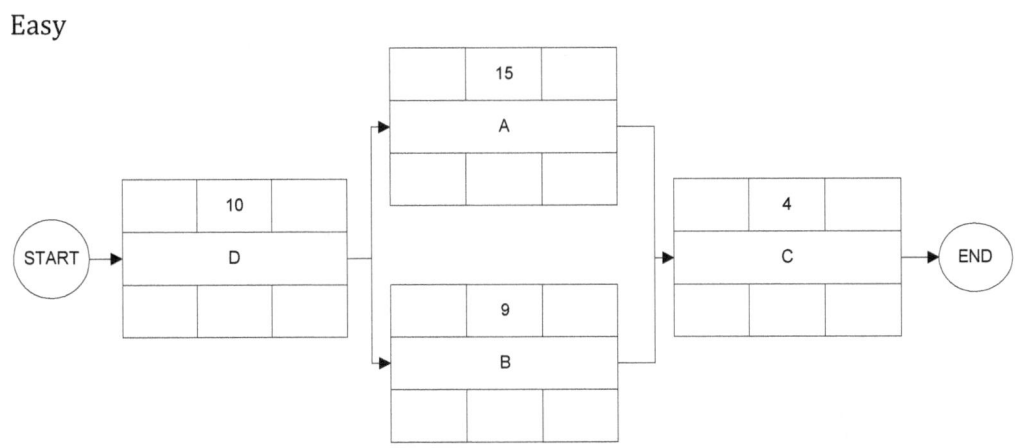

57

Moderate

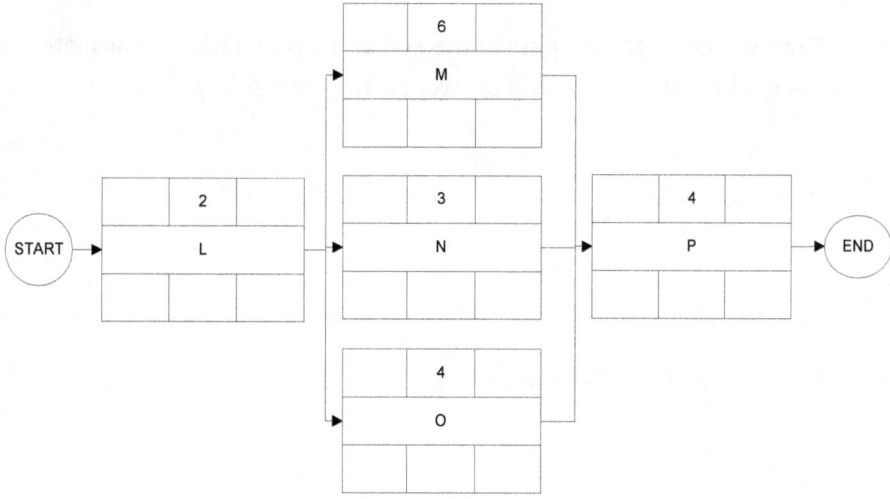

Difficult

Travel Network Diagram

Work this network diagram from the Flight Departure (END) backwards. Select any flight departure time you wish and determine what time you need to wake up from there.

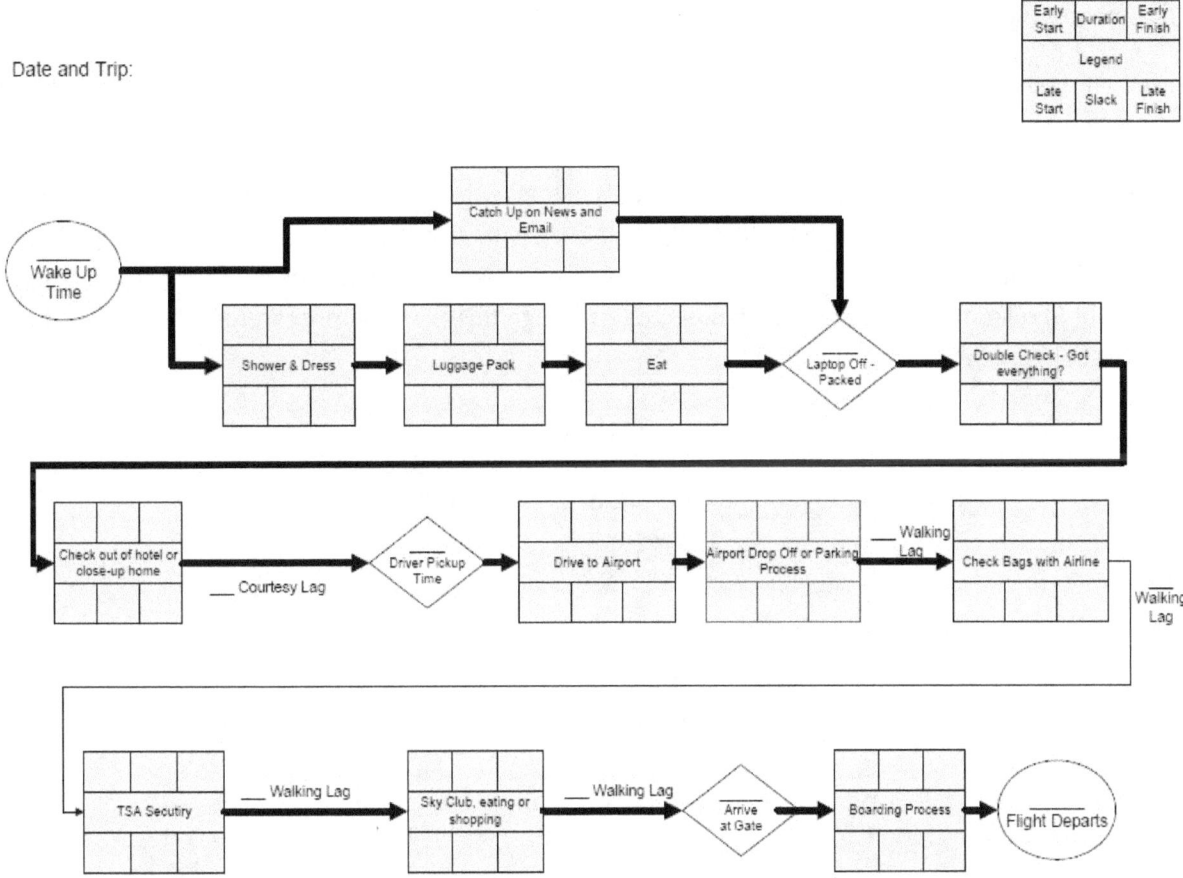

Do These Steps to Fully Prepare

Network Diagrams to Calculate from Tables:

Now the network diagramming exercises are formatted similar to what you may see on the PMP exam. To complete the following exercises, you will need to draw out the network diagram.

Based on the relationships of the work packages, draw the project network diagram from start to end. Calculate the project schedule and critical path.

You will need to be very conscientious of the details in the dependency column. Remember that a lag value greater than zero adds time to the path, while a lag with a negative value (also called a lead) reduces the time on the path. Also pay careful attention to the type of relationship. There are two Start-to-Start (S-S) relationships in Project A below. Logic through this exercise very carefully. If you need help, read the solution in the answer key.

Project A

Work Package	Duration	Dependent Upon/Relationship/Lag
A	5 weeks	Start
B	3 weeks	A, F-S
C	6 weeks	A, F-S, -1
D	2 weeks	B, S-S, + 3
E	7 weeks	D, F-S
F	5 weeks	C, F-S, -2
G	8 weeks	F, S-S, +1
H	2 weeks	F, F-S, +3
I	4 weeks	H, F-S, -1

Try another practice with many leads and lags and a start-to-start relationship below:

	Project B	
Work Package	**Duration**	**Dependent Upon/Relationship/Lag**
A	5 weeks	Start
B	3 weeks	Start
C	6 weeks	B, S-S
D	2 weeks	C, F-S, + 5
E	7 weeks	D, F-S, -1
F	5 weeks	C, F-S, +3
G	8 weeks	F, F-S, +10
H	2 weeks	E, F-S, +3
I	4 weeks	C, F-S, +12

By now you should be getting the idea. Try another project with another S-S relationship below:

	Project C	
Work Package	**Duration**	**Dependent Upon/Relationship/ Lag**
A	15 weeks	Start
B	13 weeks	A, F-S
C	16 weeks	B, F-S
D	12 weeks	C, F-S, + 5
E	17 weeks	D, S-S, -1
F	15 weeks	C, F-S

Define These Terms

Resource Optimization:

Resource Leveling:

Define these Schedule Compression terms in your own words:

Crashing:

Fast Tracking:

Section 8: Planning Processes - Cost

PLANNING PROCESS GROUP - COST

7.1 Plan Cost Management

Planning to manage, expend, and control project costs.

<u>Understand the Basics First</u>

Write the ITTO's for the process **Plan Cost Management** below:

Inputs	Tools & Techniques	Outputs
1.	1.	1.
2.	2.	
3.	3.	
4.		

In the space below. For each ITTO, if the item listed is a generic category, list at least one example that could be included:

Cost Management Plan - The Cost Management Plan establishes the prescribed precision level of cost estimates, the units of measurement that will be used to track project costs, the organizational procedures and links to account codes or accounting systems, control thresholds, earned value rules, reporting formats, and process descriptions. The plan is a guide that is used for control purposes and for comparison with actual results. The plan is expected to change during project execution due to uncertainty (risk) and requested revisions to the project plan.

Consider the **cost of quality** when determining estimates. The cost of quality includes two major components: Cost of conformance (prevention and inspection) and the cost of non-conformance (internal failure and external failure).

Reserve analysis is also used to determine project cost estimates by analyzing possible risks and determining the appropriate amount of contingency to add to project work package estimated costs.

The Cost Baseline is the aggregate of all of the estimated project costs plus the contingency reserve. The Project Budget may be greater than the Cost Baseline because it may also include an additional management reserve. The project budget is the cost baseline plus the management reserve.

This is an important concept to understand. If you find it confusing, study the helpful visual on page 255, Figure 7-9 in the PMBOK or another visual for this is as follows:

The budget contains all of the estimates and reserves. If a bottom-up estimate is being created, the budget is created from the inside of this circle out.

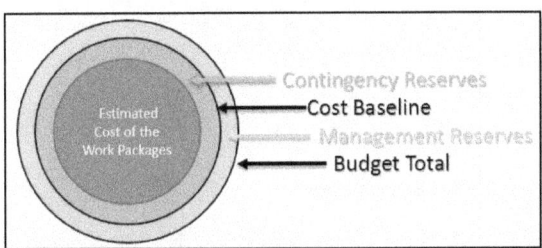

Estimation ranges vary greatly. So, when estimates are discussed it is important to define the estimates level or range of accuracy in order to set expectations accurately.

Terms of Estimate Ranges
Organizational Goals for Project Phases

Estimate Type	Range	Project Phase
Definitive	-5% to +10%	Construction
Construct	-15% to +15%	Working Drawings
Deterministic, Fixed Constraints	-20% to +50%	Design Development
Rough Order of Magnitude (ROM)	-25 to +75%	Schematic Design
Preliminary	-50% to +100%	Program Development
Concept	-30% to +120%	Feasibility Analysis
Budget, Ballpark, SWAG	-50% to +150%	Concept Review

7.2 Estimate Costs

Understand the Basics First

Write the ITTO's for the process **Estimate Costs** below:

Inputs	Tools & Techniques	Outputs
1.	1.	1.
2.	2.	2.
3.	3.	3.
4.	4.	
	5.	
	6.	
	7.	
	8.	

In the space below. For each ITTO, if the item listed is a generic category, list at least one example that could be included:

Become Better by Practicing This

Some Key **Inputs** – Project scope statement, work breakdown structure, WBS dictionary, project schedule, risk register

These are estimating **tools and techniques** that are used to produce cost estimates and a cost budget. *Define each term in your own words:*

Analogous Estimates _____

Parametric Estimates _____

Bottom-up Estimates _____

Three Point Estimating _____

Alternative Analysis _____

Reserve Analysis _____

Cost of Quality _____

Vendor Bid Analysis _____

Project Management Information System (PMIS)_____

Decision Making Techniques _____

Top down estimates will produce an estimate quickly but have a low level of reliability. Bottom up estimating is more reliable but will require more time and effort.

In some projects, initial estimates are produced using the analogous estimating technique and as the project progresses, the estimates are refined as more detail is made available. The process of adding more detail incrementally is known as progressive elaboration.

7.3 Determine Budget

Understand the Basics First

Write the ITTO's for the process **Determine Budget** below:

Inputs	Tools & Techniques	Outputs
1.	1.	1.
2.	2.	2.
3.	3.	3.
4.	4.	
5.	5.	
6.	6.	

In the space below. For each ITTO, if the item listed is a generic category, list at least one example that could be included:

Determine Budget - Apply / allocate cost estimates across project phases to create a time phased budget and a cost baseline. The Cost Baseline is used to monitor project cost performance and compare with the planned outcomes.

Cost of Quality is factor in the budget process.

Inputs - Review pages 250-251 in the *PMBOK Guide*. You will note that as you progress through the *PMBOK Guide* you will see a number of inputs that are repeated and used in many processes.

Cost Aggregation – Using the WBS, the costs estimated from the work packages are calculated and used to determine the total cost of each work package. The total costs are then aggregated up through the entire WBS to create the definitive cost estimate and project budget.

Get Better by Practicing This

Define Reserve Analysis and Management Reserves

Do These Steps to Fully Prepare

What is a Funding Limit Reconciliation? (See PMBOK section 7.3.2.5 on p. 253.) Try to restate this in your own words:

Section 9: Planning Processes (continued)

PLANNING PROCESS GROUP – QUALITY, RESOURCE, COMMUNICATIONS, RISK, PROCUREMENT, and STAKEHOLDER ENGAGEMENT

8.1 Plan Quality Management

Understand the Basics First

Write the ITTO's for the process **Plan Quality Management** below:

Inputs	Tools & Techniques	Outputs
1.	1.	1.
2.	2.	2.
3.	3.	3.
4.	4.	4.
5.	5.	
	6.	
	7.	

In the space below. For each ITTO, if the item listed is a generic category, list at least one example that could be included:

Review: Cost of Quality (COQ) – Page 282 *PMBOK® Guide and figure 8-5.*

Sigma – The term sigma means standard deviation. In our context the term is used to reference an entire quality management philosophy and methodology (Six Sigma). Conduct an Internet search to learn more about Sigma.

Quality – The degree to which a set of inherent characteristics meets full requirements. Quality is always defined by the customer. The main goal of Quality Management is customer satisfaction.

Quality Policy- Generally developed by the organization. The quality policy is an example of an organizational process asset. Project quality policies are often developed using the principles of the organization's overall operational quality policy.

The main focus is ***prevention over Inspection.*** It is less costly to prevent errors than to inspect products and deliverables and identify errors that must be corrected. It is management's responsibility to provide the resources and training that will ensure quality.

Continuous Improvement – Generally associated with the Plan, Do, Check, Act Cycle (The Shewhart Chart).

Difference Between Quality and Grade – Low or poor quality (defects, frequent repairs, missing functionality) is always unacceptable. But, low grade generally means less functionality and fewer features. A low-grade product can actually be produced at high quality.

Remember the Contributions of Quality Gurus:

	W. Deming	J.M. Juran	P. Crosby	G. Taguchi
Basic orientation toward quality	Technical	Process	Motivational	Technical, proactive
What is quality?	Nonfaulty systems	Fitness for use; freedom from trouble	Conformance to requirements	Customer's performance requirements
Goal of quality	Meet/exceed customer needs; continuous improvement	Please customer; continuous improvement	Continuous improvement; zero defects	Meet customer requirements; continuous improvement
Methods for achieving quality	Statistical; constancy of purpose; continual improvement; cooperation between functions	Cost of quality; quality trilogy: planning, control, improvement	14-point framework	Statistical methods such as Loss Function; eliminating variations of design characteristics and "noise" through robust design and processes.
Chief elements of implementation	14-point program	Breakthrough projects; quality council; quality teams	14-step program; cost of quality; quality management "maturity grid"	Statistical design of experiments (DOE); quality teams
Most famous for…	Plan ~ Do ~ Check ~ Act cycle	Responsibility for quality is on management. Very into the Pareto Principle	Zero Defects	Taguchi methodology involving prototyping.

> Draw a line to connect the Quality Guru with their associated Quality Theory
>
> | | |
> |---|---|
> | Plan ~ Do ~ Check ~ Act cycle | G. Taguchi |
> | Zero Defects | J.M. Juran |
> | Taguchi methodology involving prototyping | W. Deming |
> | Responsibility for quality is on management. Very into the Pareto Principle | P. Crosby |

ISO 9000 (International Standards Organization) – Ensures processes in place to manage the quality of deliverables produced. ISO addresses the processes not the actual output. The ISO 9000 family of quality management systems standards is designed to help organizations ensure that they meet the needs of customers and other stakeholders while meeting statutory and regulatory requirements related to a product or service.

Six Sigma – 3.4 defects per million opportunities for failure (99.99%). Other sigma values of interest are 1 sigma = 68.26%, 2 sigma = 95.46%, and 3 sigma = 99.73%. If you have difficulty remembering these percentages, make sure you have flash cards made for them.

DMAIC – Define, Measure, Analyze, Improve, Control

TQM – Total quality management: An organizational approach to quality that starts at the top management level and includes all levels of employees. The focus is on continuous improvement through training and quality improvement projects.

Quality Planning – Inputs include the scope statement and project management plan. (Remember organization process assets and enterprise environmental factors are inputs to many processes)

Cost / Benefit Analysis – Determine the level of quality to be provided, the cost to produce the level of quality, and the return on the investment.

Benchmarking – Comparing best in class to existing performance. It is the process of comparing one's business processes and performance metrics to industry bests or best practices.

Flow-charting – Diagramming a process to identify the steps involved and to identify gaps and redundant work. Flow charts are used to display and understand the overall operation of flow or work.

Design of experiments (DOE) – Developed by Taguchi. Through testing and experimenting, produce the best possible output and then repeat the defined process. According to Taguchi, quality should be built into (designed into) a product. Not inspected into it.

Cost of Quality

Review Figure 8-5 Cost of Quality on *PMBOK Guide* page 283. Our chart below displays COQ in another way and uses more common language (the cost of conformance is the cost of good quality) to make you think about it differently. Under the lowest level of this chart, note specific examples. On the exam, you may encounter example costs, which ask you to define what type of COQ the source of cost is.

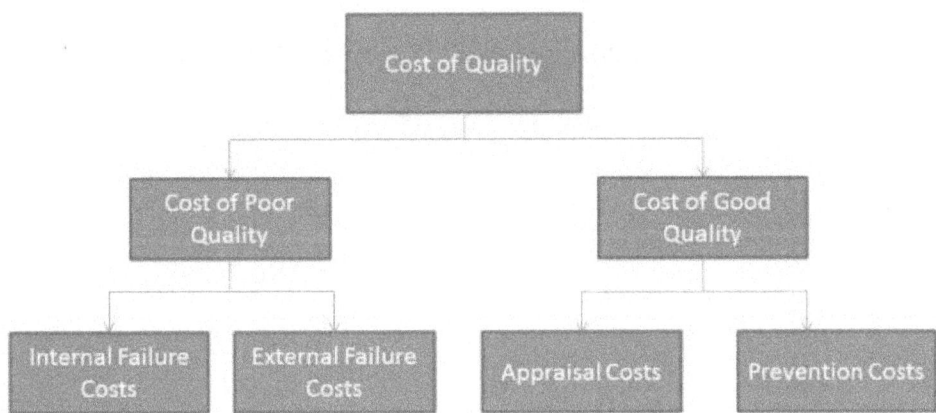

Note examples of each cost type shown above.

Become Better Prepared by Practicing This

Do you remember the values?

1 sigma = ____%
2 sigma = ____%
3 sigma = ____%
6 sigma = ____%

6 sigma levels of precision only allow for ____ defects per million.

Do These Steps to Fully Prepare

Draw a sketch in section 8.1 of our workbook.

Seven Basic Quality Tools (7QC)

1. Cause-and-effect diagram
2. Flowcharts
3. Checksheets
4. Pareto diagrams
5. Histograms
6. Control charts
7. Scatter diagrams

NOTE: The 7QC is not just a PMI or PMBOK creation, the 7QC is well known in the quality industry. It is also called ISHIKAWAS 7QC tools which was big in Japanese quality in the 1960s and 1970s. 7QC is not specifically named in the PMBOK Guide, but most of the tools are referenced individually in the PMBOK.

Draw a sketch to remind yourself what each of the 7 different tools (which are visual) look like:

9.1 Plan Resource Management

Understand the Basics First

Write the ITTO's for the process **Plan Resource Management** below:

Inputs	Tools & Techniques	Outputs
1.	1.	1.
2.	2.	2.
3.	3.	3.
4.	4.	
5.		

In the space below. For each ITTO, if the item listed is a generic category, list at least one example that could be included:

Organizational Structures are defined as Functional, Matrix, Virtual and Project Oriented. (Refer to Table 2-1 in PMBOK Guide) Define these in your own words:

Management Theories

Define these types of managers in your own words. Can you think of examples from the movies?

Theory X _____

Theory Y _____

Theory Z _____

Become Better Prepared by Practicing This

RAM – Responsibility Assignment Matrix – Links project team members with WBS tasks. The RAM is used to define clear responsibility for the completion of project tasks. It is not a tool for determining resource requirements (Page 317 PMBOK Guide).

Pre-assignment - The team has been assigned to the project before the project manager is assigned.

Negotiation - Discussing, bargaining, and developing strategies to obtain key resources and team members.

Acquisition – Contracting or outsourcing of resources.

Virtual teams – Dispersed or geographically separated project human resources. Develop strategies to keep the virtual team connected. Example – develop plans to ensure frequent and meaningful communication.

9.2 Estimate Activity Resources

Understand the Basics First

Write the ITTO's for the process **Estimate Activity Resources** below:

Inputs	Tools & Techniques	Outputs
1.	1.	1.
2.	2.	2.
3.	3.	3.
4.	4.	4.
	5.	
	6.	
	7.	

In the space below. For each ITTO, if the item listed is a generic category, list at least one example that could be included:

Become Better by Practicing This

Estimate Activity Resources uses expert judgment, alternatives analysis, published estimating data, project management software, and bottom up estimating to produce activity resource requirements. Bottom up estimating requires the use of the WBS and will produce "definitive" estimates by aggregating the information from the lowest levels of the WBS (the work packages) to the top level.

Important Inputs: Describe Resource Calendar and Risk Register

Important Tools and Techniques: Describe bottom-up resource estimating

Major Output: Describe Resource Breakdown Structure

10.1 Plan Communications Management

Plan Communications – The process of determining who needs information, what information is needed, when it is needed and in what format it will be provided.

<u>Understand the Basics First</u>

Write the ITTO's for the process **Plan Communications Management** below:

Inputs	Tools & Techniques	Outputs
1.	1.	1.
2.	2.	2.
3.	3.	3.
4.	4.	
5.	5.	
	6.	
	7.	
	8.	

In the space below. For each ITTO, if the item listed is a generic category, list at least one example that could be included:

5 C's of Communication - Refer to page 363 *PMBOK® Guide* – Communications Skills

What are the 5 C's of written communication?

Communications Requirements Analysis – Determining the specific needs of the stakeholders in terms of type of information and format (depends on the responsibility of the stakeholder) and the approach to be used to deliver information.

Communications Technology – The specific methods and media used to transfer or share information among stakeholders. Examples of communications technology include information systems and the capabilities of the stakeholders to access and send information.

Consider the urgency of the information, the availability of technology, and the length or duration of the project when determining communications requirements.

Constraints – An understanding of identified limitations that may impede communications.

Assumptions – For planning purposes, assumptions are things that are considered to be true, real, or certain. Assumptions are not based on facts and should be validated.

Communications Models - A message is encoded, transmitted, received and decoded. A feedback loop is used to ensure the message was received as intended. During the transfer of information, the message may become distorted due to "noise" (anything that may interfere with the transfer of information).

Sender–Receiver Model - Project Communications is successfully achieved through an understanding of the sender–receiver model. The sender or transmitter prepares and encodes the message. The message is subjected to distortion through different forms of noise that may interfere with the delivery and receipt of the message. The receiver decodes the message and completes the process through a feedback loop.

In the model, the critical elements are the region of experience of the sender and receiver. An overlap in regions of experience between sender and receiver or a sharing of similar background or interests will facilitate the communications process.

The sender prepares or encodes a message to transmit to a receiver. The message passes through the sender's personality screen, across the region of experience to the receiver. The message passes through the receiver's perception screen and is then decoded. To ensure that the message was received as intended the receiver will feedback the message by encoding the message, passing it through the receiver's personality screen, through to region of experience, then through the sender's perception screen. The message is decoded by the original sender to determine if the message was sent and received as intended.

Become Better by Practicing This

Communications Methods: Note an example of when each type is most appropriate:

Interactive _____

Push Communication _____

Pull Communications _____

Distribute Information: Providing the information to the stakeholders in a timely manner. Information distribution involves verbal and oral communication, listening and speaking. It includes Internal and external communication, formal and informal communication.

Communications Plan: The Communications Plan is the output to this process. Plan Content examples are found on Page 377 *PMBOK® Guide*. Use the space below to outline some of the key information that could be included in this subsidiary plan.

Do These Steps to Fully Prepare

$$N(N-1)/2$$

N = # of people on the project team

Increasing the number of people on a project team rapidly increases the number of channels of communication that will exist between project team members.

> How many channels of communication are there if there are this many people on the team:
>
> 5 people = _____ communication channels
>
> 6 people = _____ communication channels
>
> 9 people = _____ communication channels
>
> 12 people = _____ communication channels

11.1 Plan Risk Management

Risk is a measure of uncertainty. Project managers deal mainly in an area or segment of the risk spectrum known as relative uncertainty. In the risk spectrum there are very few risk events that have a 0% probability of occurring and very few items that have a 100% chance of occurring.

Understand the Basics First

Write the ITTO's for the process **Plan Risk Management** below:

Inputs	Tools & Techniques	Outputs
1.	1.	1.
2.	2.	
3.	3.	
4.		
5.		

In the space below. For each ITTO, if the item listed is a generic category, list at least one example that could be included:

Define Risks and Issues – what are the differences?

Known Unknown – Some information is available and can be planned for to some extent. Contingencies are developed to manage known unknowns.

Unknown Unknown – No information is available, you cannot plan for something that is not known at all. Management reserves are created to deal with risk events that cannot be identified and planned for.

Risk management considers **threats** as well as **opportunities** - positive side of risk and the negative side of risk.

There are two primary components of Risk – **Probability and Impact.** A third component sometimes considered is **Urgency**. Urgency may be used as a factor to further the process of risk event prioritization.

Risk Appetite – Degree of uncertainty an entity is willing to take on.

Risk Tolerance – The Utility factor: Generally used to describe how risk affects an organization or an individual. Utility rises at a decreasing rate for the risk adverse organization (meaning that as risk or the costs associated with risk increases the reaction or response to the risk situation becomes less positive). Utility increases for the risk seeker (as the potential severity of the risk increase the reaction becomes more and more positive). Risk seekers thrive on risk opportunities (they like taking risks).

Consider the culture of an organization as it relates to risk management (risk takers vs. risk adverse organizations) Risk tolerance is an example of an enterprise environmental factor.

Risk Triggers – Symptoms that may lead to a risk event. React to triggers before a risk event occurs.

Types of Risks:

- Insurable Risk – Chance for loss only
- Business Risk - Chance for profit or loss

The Risk Management Plan includes Methodology, Roles and Responsibilities, Budgeting, Timing, Risk Categories, and the Risk Breakdown Structure. Are you considering these for your projects?

Define the relationship between overall project risk and project timing:

Become Better Prepared by Reviewing This

Hurwitz and Wald Criterion – Hurwitz criterion is known as Maximax and is considered to be a "Go for broke" attitude. It is an optimistic outlook with the expectation that eventually there will be a win or a positive outcome. This criterion is generally associated with organizations possessing significant assets and cash reserves.

Wald criterion or Maximin is concerned mainly with potential loss. Organizational Managers who are associated with this risk attitude are generally considered to be risk averse and are concerned about how much will be lost.

11.2 Identify Risks

Understand the Basics First

Write the ITTO's for the process **Identify Risks** below:

Inputs	Tools & Techniques	Outputs
1.	1.	1.
2.	2.	2.
3.	3.	3.
4.	4.	
5.	5.	
6.	6.	

In the space below. For each ITTO, if the item listed is a generic category, list at least one example that could be included:

Risk Identification – Information Gathering Techniques Review

Determining which risks might affect the project and documenting the characteristics.

- Brainstorming – Gathering risk data from the project team by openly generating ideas.
- Delphi – Use of subject matter experts in an anonymous setting to eliminate bias.
- Nominal Group technique – The information is gathered by the group and then voted on. Voting is anonymous to minimize influence and bias, but the participants are known to all.
- SWOT – Strengths, Weaknesses, Opportunities, Threats.
- Root Cause analysis – Use of fishbone or Ishikawa diagram.
- Risk Categories – Use of a Risk Breakdown Structure. Typical categories include: Technical. Organizational, External, and Project management.
- Risk Register – An organized and prioritized list of risks with details about root causes, probability and impact, and responses to the risks.
- Risk Breakdown Structure _____
- Risk Register _____

Become Better Prepared by Practicing This

Draw a line connecting the risk information gathering process with its correct description. See *PMBOK® Guide* section 11.2.2 *Identify Risks: Tools and Techniques* to check your answers.

Process	Match by drawing lines	Description
Delphi Technique		Talking with experienced project experts, including project team members, stakeholders, and subject matter experts and getting their help in identifying risks.
Brainstorming		This technique examines the project from each of the strengths, weaknesses, opportunities, and threats perspectives. The analysis also examines the degree to which organizational strengths may offset threats and determines if weaknesses might hinder opportunities.
Interviewing		This technique is facilitated either free-form or as a structured mass interview. In this technique people are encouraged to be open minded and non-judgmental to obtain a comprehensive list of project risks.
Root Cause Analysis		An information gathering technique used as a way to reach consensus of experts on a subject. Experts on the subject participate in this technique anonymously. A facilitator uses a questionnaire to solicit ideas about the important project points related to the subject. The responses are summarized and are then re-circulated to the experts for further comment. Consensus may be reached in a few rounds of this process. This technique helps reduce bias in the data and keeps any one person from having undue influence on the outcome.
SWOT Analysis		This is a very specific technique used to identify a problem, discover the underlying causes that lead to it, and develop preventive action.

11.3 Perform Qualitative Risk Analysis

Understand the Basics First

Write the ITTO's for the process **Perform Qualitative Risk Analysis** below:

Inputs	Tools & Techniques	Outputs
1.	1.	1.
2.	2.	
3.	3.	
4.	4.	
	5.	
	6.	
	7.	

In the space below. For each ITTO, if the item listed is a generic category, list at least one example that could be included:

Types of Scales

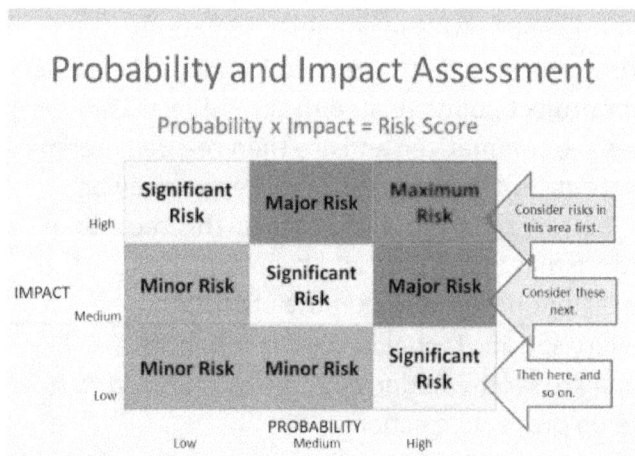

Nominal scales are simply labels with no overlap, such as categories of risk which could include safety, public relations, or financial.

Ordinal scales rank data in order of magnitude since there is no standard of measurement for differences: for instance, a risk matrix that shows low, medium, and high.

86

Cardinal scales are actual numeric or score values assigned to risks.

11.4 Perform Quantitative Risk Analysis

Quantitative Risk analysis converts risk scores into much more detailed estimated monetary values and performs probability analysis. It uses tools such as sensitivity analysis, decision trees and Monte Carlo simulation.

<u>Understand the Basics First</u>

Write the ITTO's for the process **Perform Quantitative Risk Analysis** below:

Inputs	Tools & Techniques	Outputs
1.	1.	1.
2.	2.	
3.	3.	
4.	4.	
	5.	

In the space below. For each ITTO, if the item listed is a generic category, list at least one example that could be included:

<u>Get Better by Practicing This</u>

Probability Distributions: Draw a sketch for these: Beta, Normal, Uniform, Triangular

Define Sensitivity Analysis in your own words:

Expected monetary value (EMV) – The product of probability and impact. Decision Trees provide a mechanism for determining the expected monetary value of a choice or direction. Expected monetary value is calculated on a decision tree by considering the cost of each decision, the probability of an outcome, and the net path value. See page 435 in the *PMBOK® Guide* 6th edition for a detailed explanation.

Decision trees: The decision tree is associated with Quantitative Risk Analysis. They are used to assist in the process determining a direction to take by considering the implications of each of the available alternatives.

Modeling and Simulation -Monte Carlo Process: Simulation of a project using software to run the project many times to determine possible outcomes and probability of meeting project objectives. Examples of software with Monte Carlo capabilities include Risk Plus, @Risk, and Monte Carlo plugins for Excel.

Standard Deviation – Used to determine confidence level. Generally accepted formula for standard deviation for the exam is:

$$(b-a) / 6 \text{ where b (pessimistic) minus a (optimistic) divided by 6.}$$

As an option, this formula may be derived from the weighted average formula or PERT estimate:

$$\{\text{Optimistic value} + 4 \text{ times (most likely value)} + \text{pessimistic value}\} / 6$$

<u>Do These Steps to Fully Prepare</u>

Residual risks are those that are expected to remain after planned responses have been taken, as well as those that have been deliberately accepted. List some examples of your own:

Secondary risk – A risk that develops as a result of the implementation of a risk response to a primary risk. List some examples of your own:

11.5 Plan Risk Responses

Understand the Basics First

Write the ITTO's for the process **Plan Risk Responses** below:

Inputs	Tools & Techniques	Outputs
1.	1.	1.
2.	2.	2.
3.	3.	3.
4.	4.	
	5.	
	6.	
	7.	
	8.	
	9.	

In the space below. For each ITTO, if the item listed is a generic category, list at least one example that could be included:

Risk Response Strategies

For threats and opportunities: The acceptance response can be active or passive. Types of acceptance are:

1. **Passive acceptance** – Generally this means that no special action will be taken until a risk event occurs
2. **Active acceptance** – This means planning for the risk event by developing a specific contingency (Basically, taking action to address a potential risk situation that has been accepted).

Define Contingent Response in your own words. (Reference PMBOK p. 445.)

Become Better Prepared by Practicing This

List and describe the 5 negative risk strategies and the 5 positive risk strategies from memory. Make sure you know these. If you cannot easily recall them, make flashcards now.

Negative 1	Positive 1
Negative 2	Positive 2
Negative 3	Positive 3
Negative 4	Positive 4
Negative 5	Positive 5

12.1 Plan Procurement Management

Understand the Basics First

Write the ITTO's for the process **Plan Procurement Management** below:

Inputs	Tools & Techniques	Outputs
1.	1.	1.
2.	2.	2.
3.	3.	3.
4.	4.	4.
5.	5.	5.
6..		6.
		7.
		8.
		9.
		10.

In the space below. For each ITTO, if the item listed is a generic category, list at least one example that could be included:

Become Better by Practicing This

Types of Contracts – Page 471 PMBOK Guide

As a buyer, when would you use these contract types?

Fixed Price

_____
_____

Cost-reimbursable

_____
_____

Time and Material

_____
_____

Fixed Price Incentive Fee

_____
_____

Cost Plus Incentive Fee

_____
_____

Define Point of Total Assumption in your own words:

_____
_____

Note: It is very important that you understand this concept of the PTA for the PMP exam, as it has appeared a number of times in the past on the test.

Practice this formula: ((Target cost – Actual Cost) * Seller's sharing ratio) + Target fee

Target Cost (what the project is estimated to cost not including sellers profit): $2,000,000
Target Profit: $200,000
Target Price (target cost + target fee): $2,200,000
Ceiling Price: $2,450,000
Share Ratio: 80% buyer/20% seller for overruns
50/50% for underruns

Do These Steps to Fully Prepare

Read about these contracts and utilize the contract clues to help you study for the exam:

	Type	What it Is	Example	Primary Used For	Advantages	Disadvantages	Risk
CPIF	Cost Plus Incentive Fee	Buyer pays all costs, a fixed fee, plus a bonus for beating target costs	Cost + 10% Target Fee (50/50 Sharing Ratio)	-Best when buyer is purchasing expertise in determining all that needs to be done -Used for long duration or R&D type projects	-Minimizes negotiations and preliminary specification costs -Easier/faster for the buyer to prepare the contract statement of work -Contractor motivated to limit costs	-Requires buyer to audit seller cost -No assurance of actual final cost	**Risk to Buyer:** Medium **Risk to Seller:** Medium
CPFF	Cost Plus Fixed Fee	Buyer pays for all costs plus a pre-determined fixed fee	Cost + $25,000 as a fee	-Best when buyer is purchasing expertise in determining all that needs to be done	- Minimizes negotiations and preliminary specification costs -Easier/faster for the buyer to prepare the contract statement of work	- Seller only has limited incentive to manage costs -Requires buyer to audit seller cost -No assurance of actual final cost	**Risk to Buyer:** High **Risk to Seller:** Low
T&M	Time and Material	Buyer pays per hour or per item charge. Contains elements of both a fixed price and cost reimburse-able contract	$150 per hour plus expenses	-Used primarily for small projects and when buyer is hiring resources to augment staff	-Allows for work to begin quickly	-Seller earns increased profit from increased duration	**Risk to Buyer:** Medium **Risk to Seller:** Medium
FFP	Firm Fixed Price	Buyer pays an agreed upon cost for all of the work	$50,000	-Best when buyer has definite requirements and specifications	-Requires less administrative effort for both buyer and seller -Seller has high incentive to manage costs	-More work for the buyer to write Statement of Work (SOW)	**Risk to Buyer:** Very Low **Risk to Seller:** Very High
FPI	Fixed Price Incentive	Buyer and seller share savings underneath amount baselined in contract	$100,000 + $1000 per week completed ahead of schedule $100,000 Target Price + $10,000 Target Fee (40/60 Sharing Ratio)	-Best when buyer has definite requirements and specifications. -Buyer motivated for early project completion.	-Requires less administrative effort for both buyer and seller -Seller has high incentive to manage costs	-More work for the buyer to write Statement of Work (SOW)	**Risk to Buyer:** Low **Risk to Seller:** High

13.2 Plan Stakeholder Engagement

Understand the Basics First

Write the ITTO's for the process **Plan Stakeholder Engagement** below:

Inputs	Tools & Techniques	Outputs
1.	1.	1.
2.	2.	.
3.	3.	
4.	4.	
5.	5.	
6.	6.	

In the space below. For each ITTO, if the item listed is a generic category, list at least one example that could be included:

Become Better by Practicing This

Stakeholder Management Plan – Page 522 *PMBOK Guide*
Describe what the Stakeholder Management plan provides:

Do These Steps to Fully Prepare

In a **Stakeholder Engagement Matrix**, if the stakeholders are listed on the Y axis, what are the five likely engagement levels that would be on the X axis? Write them in the cells to the right of the "Stakeholder" corner box. Then check your work against Figure 13-6 on p. 522 of the *PMBOK® Guide*.

Stakeholder					
Stakeholder 1					
Stakeholder 2					
Stakeholder 3					

Section 10: Executing Process Group

EXECUTING PROCESS GROUP

4.3 Direct and Manage Project Work
This is where you get the work done that you have been planning.

Understand the Basics First

Write the ITTO's for the process **Direct and Manage Project Work** below:

Inputs	Tools & Techniques	Outputs
1.	1.	1.
2.	2.	2.
3.	3.	3.
4.		4.
5.		5.
		6.
		7.

In the space below. For each ITTO, if the item listed is a generic category, list at least one example that could be included:

Work Performance Data is an output. The work you are performing during execution is creating work performance data. Through your monitoring and controlling activities you will turn this data into actionable information which you will share through work performance reporting.

DIRECT AND MANAGE PROJECT WORK	WORK PERFORMANCE DATA	MONITORING AND CONTROLLING	WORK PERFORMANCE INFORMATION	WORK PERFORMANCE REPORTS

4.4 Manage Project Knowledge

Process of using existing knowledge and creating new knowledge to achieve the project's objectives and contribute to organizational learning.

Understand the Basics First

Write the ITTO's for the process 4.4 **Manage Project Knowledge** below:

Inputs	Tools & Techniques	Outputs
1.	1.	1.
2.	2.	2.
3.	3.	3.
4.	4.	
5.		

In the space below. For each ITTO, if the item listed is a generic category, list at least one example that could be included:

Become Better by Practicing This

Fill in the blanks:

The most important part of knowledge management is creating an atmosphere of _____ so that people are motivated to _____ their _____.

Do These Steps to Fully Prepare

Knowledge Management vs Information Management – Knowledge and Information are terms that are commonly interchanged. What does the PMBOK share about the difference between these two terms?

8.2 Manage Quality
Understand the Basics First

Write the ITTO's for the process **Manage Quality** below:

Inputs	Tools & Techniques	Outputs
1.	1.	1.
2.	2.	2.
3.	3.	3.
	4.	4.
	5.	5.
	6.	
	7.	
	8.	

In the space below. For each ITTO, if the item listed is a generic category, list at least one example that could be included:

Quality Management ensures that an organization, product or service is consistent. It has four main components: **quality** planning, **quality** assurance, **quality** control and **quality** improvement. **Quality management** is focused not only on product and service **quality**, but also on the means to achieve it.

Quality Assurance – Systematic activities implemented to ensure that the project will satisfy quality standards. QA tools include audits and process analysis. Quality assurance is generally associated with establishing processes that will assist in managing the outputs of an action or maintaining consistency of deliverables.

Become Better Prepared by Practicing This

Many students have difficulty differentiating between manage quality, also known as, quality assurance and quality control. This chart provides a contrasting analysis:

	Quality Assurance	**Quality Control**
Definition	QA is a set of activities for ensuring quality in the processes by which products are developed.	QC is a set of activities for ensuring quality in products. The activities focus on identifying defects in the actual products produced.
Focus on	QA aims to prevent defects with a focus on the process used to make the product. It is a proactive quality process.	QC aims to identify (and correct) defects in the finished product. Quality control, therefore, is a reactive process.
Goal	The goal of QA is to improve development and test processes so that defects do not arise when the product is being developed.	The goal of QC is to identify defects after a product is developed and before it's released.
How	Establish a good quality management system and the assessment of its adequacy. Periodic conformance audits of the operations of the system.	Finding & eliminating sources of quality problems through tools & equipment so that customer's requirements are continually met.
What	Prevention of quality problems through planned and systematic activities including documentation.	The activities or techniques used to achieve and maintain the product quality, process and service.
Responsibility	Everyone on the team involved in developing the product is responsible for quality assurance.	Quality control is usually the responsibility of a specific team that tests the product for defects.
Example	Verification is an example of QA.	Validation/Software Testing is an example of QC.
As a tool	QA is a managerial tool.	QC is a corrective tool.

9.3 Acquire Resources
Understand the Basics First

Write the ITTO's for the process **Acquire Resources** below:

Inputs	Tools & Techniques	Outputs
1.	1.	1.
2.	2.	2.
3.	3.	3.
4.	4.	4.
		5.
		6.
		7.
		8.

In the space below. For each ITTO, if the item listed is a generic category, list at least one example that could be included:

Use a **staffing pool or resource pool** if available. The goal is to obtain the best resources available. In most cases, the project team is comprised of competent performers who can complete the work required with moderate levels of supervision and coaching.

Negotiating – Project managers must develop effective negotiating skills to successfully achieve project objectives. Items that may require negotiation include: resources, schedules, activity duration estimates, project funding, activity cost estimate.

9.4 Develop Team
Understand the Basics First

Write the ITTO's for the process for the **Develop Team** process below:

Inputs	Tools & Techniques	Outputs
1.	1.	1.
2.	2.	2.
3.	3.	3.
4.	4.	4.
	5.	5.
	6.	6.
	7.	
	8.	

In the space below. For each ITTO, if the item listed is a generic category, list at least one example that could be included:

Team Development – The project manager is a team leader and should determine the best methods to enhance the performance of the team. Consider these opportunities for team development:

1. Team building activities
2. Reward and recognition
3. Training, appraisals, and feedback
4. Co-location

Stages of team conflict and team development

Forming – Storming – Norming – Performing is a model of group development, first proposed by Bruce Tuckman in 1965, who maintained that these phases are all necessary and inevitable in order for the team to grow, to face up to challenges, to tackle problems, to find solutions, to plan work, and to deliver results. Adjourning is a phase that was later added to apply to project teams.

Conflict begins during the forming of the team, it intensives during the storming phase, begins to subside in the norming phase, and is minimized in the performing stage. Conflict may be present throughout the project life cycle and can actually be beneficial if managed properly.

9.5 Manage Team
Understand the Basics First

Inputs	Tools & Techniques	Outputs
1.	1.	1.
2.	2.	2.
3.		3.
4.		4.
5.		
6.		

In the space below. For each ITTO, if the item listed is a generic category, list at least one example that could be included:

Power – There are generally 5 types of Personal Power – Formal or legitimate, Reward, Penalty, Expert, Referent.

Conflict – Remember the different types of Conflict handling modes – Withdrawal, Smoothing, Compromise, Forcing, and Collaboration / Confrontation. Learn what each of them means.

Motivation – Douglas McGregor classified managers as Theory X or Y. Ouchi's Theory Z grew on that.

- Theory X – A micro-manager, distrusts employees, believes employees do not want to work and will do only what is minimally required
- Theory Y – Participative style, trusting, supportive. Believes people want to work and make a contribution.
- Theory Z – Ouchi. Focus on the greater good of the organization. Less attention to individual needs. Organizational goals are important. Ouchi taught that high levels of trust, confidence, and commitment with workers lead to high levels of support of the organization's goals.

Maslow's Hierarchy of Needs

As each motivating factor is achieved it is no longer considered a motivator. The 5 levels are:

1. Physiological needs – Lowest Level of the hierarchy.
2. Safety and Security
3. Social needs
4. Esteem
5. Self-actualization

Herzberg's Hygiene Theory

First it is important to remove or address the items that can cause dissatisfaction and establish a good working environment, then focus on motivators such as greater challenges, more responsibility, advancement, reward and recognition.

<u>Get Better by Practicing This</u>

Review the Composition of Project Teams

<u>Dedicated teams</u> and <u>part-time teams</u> can exist in any of the organizational structures.

However, dedicated project teams are most often seen in which type of organization?

And part-time project teams are very common in which type of organization?

10.2 Manage Communications

Understand the Basics First

Write the ITTO's for the process **Manage Communications** below:

Inputs	Tools & Techniques	Outputs
1.	1.	1.
2.	2.	2.
3.	3.	3.
4.	4.	4.
5.	5.	
	6.	
	7.	

In the space below. For each ITTO, if the item listed is a generic category, list at least one example that could be included:

Become Better Prepared by Practicing This

There are some philosophies about communications that are not described in the *PMBOK® Guide* that you will need to familiarize yourself with. Spend 5 minutes researching each of these topics and end by filling in the sender/receiver communication model shown on the next page.

1. When are different **levels of formality** appropriate in communicating via different methods (in writing versus orally, in person versus email, a formal report versus an informal memo, etc)?

2. **Writing style**: Describe active voice versus passive voice and indicate when each is appropriate.

3. What are **meeting management** best practices?

4. What are **presentation best practices**?

5. What are **good techniques for building consensus** and overcoming obstacles in a group?

6. What are best practices for **active and accurate listening**?

Do These Steps to Fully Prepare

Sender/receiver communication model

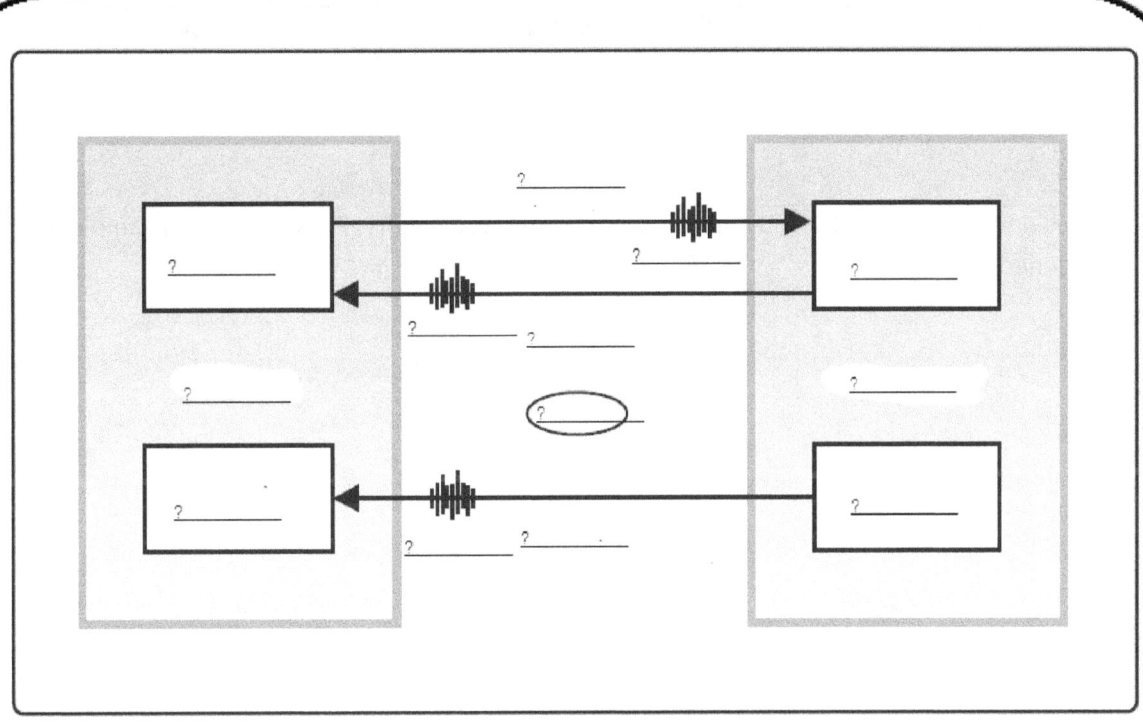

Fill in each blank above for the communication model found in Figure 10.4 on p. 373 in the *PMBOK® Guide*.

11.6 Implement Risk Responses
Understand the Basics First - ITTO Table

Write the ITTO's for the process **Conduct Procurements** below:

Inputs	Tools & Techniques	Outputs
1.	1.	1.
2.	2.	2.
3.	3.	

In the space below. For each ITTO, if the item listed is a generic category, list at least one example that could be included:

Become Better by Practicing This

Implement Risk Responses ensures that agreed upon risk responses are executed as planned in order to address overall project risk exposure, minimize individual project threats, and maximize individual project opportunities. This process is performed throughout the project.

Complete the following statement:

A common problem with Project Risk Management is that project teams spend effort, _____ then risk responses are agreed upon and documented in, _____ but _____.

12.2 Conduct Procurements

Understand the Basics First - ITTO Table

Write the ITTO's for the process **Conduct Procurements** below:

Inputs	Tools & Techniques	Outputs
1.	1.	1.
2.	2.	2.
3.	3.	3.
4.	4.	4.
5.	5.	5.
6.		6.

In the space below. For each ITTO, if the item listed is a generic category, list at least one example that could be included:

Become Better Prepared by Practicing This

Remember the advantages and disadvantages of the different types of contracts:

- FFP – Firm Fixed Price or Lump Sum – Greater risk to seller
- Cost Plus Fixed Fee – All additional costs assumed by the buyer
- Cost Plus Percentage of Cost – Seller receives a percentage of all project costs
- Cost Plus Incentive Fee – Seller attempts to keep costs under target and receives a percentage of the savings
- Fixed Price Incentive Fee – Ceiling price is negotiated (Fixed price) and the seller attempts to complete at lowest cost. Seller receives a percentage of cost savings in addition to the negotiated profit.

Incentive Contracts - Some contracts include a sharing ratio between the buyer and the seller. The incentive is designed to encourage the seller to control and reduce cost. In these types of arrangements, the buyer and seller can benefit by sharing the savings.

The FPIF contract includes cost and price points, a ratio, and a formula. They include:

- **Target Cost (TC):** The initially negotiated figure for estimated contract costs and the point at which profit pivots.
- **Target Profit (TP):** The initially negotiated profit at the target cost.
- **Target Price:** Target cost plus the target profit.
- **Ceiling Price (CP):** Stated as a percent of the target cost, this is the maximum price the buyer expects to pay. Once this amount is reached, the seller pays all remaining costs for the original work.
- **Share Ratio (SR):** The buyer/seller sharing ratio for cost savings or cost overruns that will increase or decrease the actual profit. The buyer percentage is listed first, and the terms used are "buyer share" and "seller share." For example, on an 80/20 share ratio, the buyer's share is 80 percent and the seller's share is 20 percent.
- **Point of Total Assumption (PTA):** The point where cost increases that exceed the target cost are no longer shared by the buyer according to the share ratio. At this point, the seller's profit is reduced one dollar for every additional dollar of cost. **PTA = ((Ceiling Price - Target Price)/buyer's Share Ratio) + Target Cost**

Remember the respective risks to the buyer and the seller relative to contract type.

Firm Fixed Price Contract (FFP) – Increased risk for the seller. Seller usually includes a contingency reserve in the final price as a buffer for unexpected costs.

Cost Plus – Increased risk for the buyer. This type of contract is generally associated with situations where the buyer is uncertain about requirements and a significant amount of change may occur. The costs associated with the changes are assumed by the buyer.

Incentive Contracts – Contracts of this type include a sharing ratio negotiated between the buyer and seller. If costs are kept below target, the amount of savings is shared between the buyer and seller. The formula for a cost plus incentive fee is **((Target cost – Actual Cost) * Seller's sharing ratio) + Target fee**

Contract Components: The key items that form a contract

- An offer
- An acceptance
- A consideration (something of value)
- A contract is a legal document that is remediated in court.

Other types of Contracts – Time and Material, Purchase Order, Letter Contract or Letter of Intent

The Letter of Intent, or Letter Contract, allows the seller to begin work while final approvals for the actual contract are being processed. This prevents the project from experiencing start up delays.

The Definitive Contract – This is the final, approved contract that describes the expected outcome and deliverables.

Procurement Documents – Request for Proposal (RFP), Request for Information (RFI), Request for Bid (RFB), Request for Quotation (RFQ), Invitation for Bid (IFB).

Statement of Work (SOW) – A narrative description of work to be completed under contract. Details the work to be done by the contractor and allows the contractor to determine if the work can be performed.

Make or Buy Decisions – Determining whether or not to purchase goods and services, obtain them, or make them internally using organizational resources, equipment and capacity. The key element here is to consider the benefits and disadvantages of the make or buy decision.

Rent or Buy or Rent vs. Lease – Must be able to determine the break-even point. This process assists in determining the most cost-effective approach when deciding on the purchase or resources and support for the project.

Example – Rent a piece of equipment for $100 per day or lease the equipment for $60 per day plus a $5000 one-time cost. What is the break-even point?

> Solve for the number of days: X = Days 100x = $5000 + $60X
> 100x – 60x = 5000
> 40x = 5000
> X = 5000/40
> X = 125

Bidder Conference – An important element in the procurement process – Scheduled and facilitated by the buyer, it provides a level playing field for potential contractors, information about the project and the desired work is provided to all interested contractors.

Negotiation – Location and environment are critical elements. Consider the needs of each party including issues such as room size, table shape, location, positioning of each participant. Understand the opposing view point. Consider the minimum that will be accepted and the maximum that will be offered (min-max).

Weighting System – Used to select a seller. Sellers are scored using various criteria. A weighting factor is used for each specific criterion.

Screening – Used to ensure minimum qualifications of the seller.

Special Terms and Conditions:

- Penalty clauses
- Liquidated damages – damages that are designated during the contract negotiations that specify compensation amounts upon a specific breach of contract (e.g., late performance).
- Waiver – A waiver is the voluntary or surrender of some known right or privilege.
- Non-Disclosure Agreement – Protecting the proprietary information of an organization.

- Arbitration – Using an independent third party to settle disputes without going to court. The third party acting as arbitrator must be agreed by both sides. Contracts often include arbitration clauses nominating an arbitrator in advance.
- Breach of contract – Failure by one party to a contract to uphold their part of the deal. A breach of contract will make the whole contract void and can lead to damages being awarded against the party which is in breach.
- Collective agreement – Term used for agreements made between employees and employers, usually involving trade unions. They often cover more than one organization. Although these can be seen as contracts, they are governed by employment law, not contract law.
- Incentives – Contracts may have provisions that will provide incentives to the buyer and the seller. Example– Fixed Price plus incentive (FFPI). In these contracts a sharing ratio is established between the buyer and seller that will provide some type of incentive to keep costs down or to complete the project early.
- Termination for convenience – No longer need the product or service. Generally decided by the buyer.
- Termination due to default – Failure of the contractor to provide a satisfactory deliverable.
- Force Majeure (acts of God, strikes, etc.) – This normal contract clause protects the seller from liabilities and penalties when a project is impacted by a natural disaster.
- Privity – The doctrine of privity in contract law provides that a contract cannot confer rights or impose obligations arising under it on any person or agent except the parties to it.

Types of contract changes:

1. Administrative change – Records only, example: change of billing address
2. Constructive change – Impacts the actual work. Example: Customer supplied equipment or property is not available on the date scheduled. This usually requires re-planning and changes to the work schedule and other activities.

Project Reviews – Procurement and quality audits, should be done on a regular basis

Close-out – Punch lists, verification of contracted deliverables, formal acceptance, post project review, contract reviews.

Example of a FPIF contract – Fixed Price Incentive Fee

Target cost = 100,000, Target fee = 10,000. Target price = 110,000, Ceiling price = 130,000, Sharing Ratio 80/20 – 80% to buyer, 20% to seller. Actual cost = 90,000, Cost savings = 10,000, .20 x 10,000 = 2000 (share to be received by the seller).

Point of Total Assumption (PTA): The point where cost increases that exceed the target cost are no longer shared by the government according to the share ratio. At this point, the seller's profit is reduced one dollar for every additional dollar of cost.

Do These Steps to Fully Prepare

Fill in what the risk to the buyer and seller is for each type (very low, low, medium, high, or very high).

	Type	What it Is	Example	Primary Used For	Advantages	Disadvantages	Cost Risk
CPIF	Cost Plus Incentive Fee	Buyer pays all costs, a fixed fee, plus a bonus for beating target costs	Cost + 10% Target Fee (50/50 Sharing Ratio)	- Best when buyer is purchasing expertise in determining all that needs to be done - Used for long duration or R&D type projects	- Minimizes negotiations and preliminary specification costs - Easier/faster for the buyer to prepare the contract statement of work - Contractor motivated to limit costs	- Requires buyer to audit seller cost - No assurance of actual final cost	Risk to Buyer: _____ Risk to Seller: _____
CPFF	Cost Plus Fixed Fee	Buyer pays for all costs plus a pre-determined fixed fee	Cost + $25,000 as a fee	-Best when buyer is purchasing expertise in determining all that needs to be done	- Minimizes negotiations and preliminary specification costs -Easier/faster for the buyer to prepare the contract statement of work	- Seller only has limited incentive to manage costs -Requires buyer to audit seller cost -No assurance of actual final cost	Risk to Buyer: _____ Risk to Seller: _____
T&M	Time and Material	Buyer pays per hour or per item charge. Contains elements of both a fixed price and cost reimburse-able contract	$150 per hour plus expenses	-Used primarily for small projects and when buyer is hiring resources to augment staff	-Allows for work to begin quickly	-Seller earns increased profit from increased duration	Risk to Buyer: _____ Risk to Seller: _____
CPPC	Cost Plus Percentage Cost	Buyer pays for all costs plus a percent of costs as the fee	Cost + 10% of costs as a fee	-Not allowed in government contracting	-No advantages for the buyer	-Sellers are not motivated to control costs because they directly benefit from increased cost	Risk to Buyer: _____ Risk to Seller: _____
FFP	Firm Fixed Price	Buyer pays an agreed upon cost for all of the work	$50,000	-Best when buyer has definite requirements and specifications	-Requires less administrative effort for both buyer and seller -Seller has high incentive to manage costs	-More work for the buyer to write Statement of Work (SOW)	Risk to Buyer: _____ Risk to Seller: _____
FPI	Fixed Price Incentive	Buyer and seller share savings underneath amount baselined in contract	$100,000 + $1,000 per week completed ahead of schedule $100,000 Target Price + $10,000 Target Fee (40/60 Sharing Ratio)	-Best when buyer has definite requirements and specifications. -Buyer motivated for early project completion.	-Requires less administrative effort for both buyer and seller -Seller has high incentive to manage costs	-More work for the buyer to write Statement of Work (SOW)	Risk to Buyer: _____ Risk to Seller: _____

13.3 Manage Stakeholder Engagement

Understand the Basics First

Involves communicating and working with stakeholders to meet their expectations.

Write the ITTO's for the process **Manage Stakeholder Engagement** below:

Inputs	Tools & Techniques	Outputs
1.	1.	1.
2.	2.	2.
3.	3.	3.
4.	4.	
	5.	

In the space below. For each ITTO, if the item listed is a generic category, list at least one example that could be included:

Interpersonal skills – Building trust, resolving conflict, active listening, overcoming resistance to change.

Management skills – Set and manage objectives, influencing people, negotiating agreements, managing and modifying organizational behavior.

Communications Models – 10.1.2.4 page 371-373 *PMBOK Guide*.

Note examples of each form of communication:

Interactive communications _____

Push communications _____

Pull communications _____

Become Better Prepared by Practicing This

Study Figure 13-8 Manage Stakeholder Engagement Data Flow Diagram on p. 524 of the PMBOK.

1. Thinking about the flow, imagine a scenario where a stakeholder tells you that their expectations are not being met by the project team. Think about what would happen if you did not find an effective way to quickly and professionally communicate that to the project team.

Section 11: Monitoring and Controlling Process Group

Monitoring and Controlling focuses on the assessment of project performance. The project manager compares planned results with actual results to determine where variances may exist. In this process group, the project manager and team identify unfavorable variances and new risks. They track existing risks and how the responses to those risks are affecting the project. Status of the project (typically described as red, green, or amber) is prepared and delivered to stakeholders. Changes are managed through an approved and enforced change control process.

MONITORING AND CONTROLLING PROCESS GROUP

4.5 Monitor and Control Project Work

Understand the Basics First

Write the ITTO's for the process **Monitor and Control Project Work** below:

Inputs	Tools & Techniques	Outputs
1.	1.	1.
2.	2.	2.
3.	3.	3.
4.	4.	4.
5.		
6.		

In the space below. For each ITTO, if the item listed is a generic category, list at least one example that could be included:

Become Better Prepared by Practicing This

Study Figure 4-11. Monitor and Control Project Work Data Flow Diagram on p. 106 of the *PMBOK Guide*.

- Pay special attention to the flow of Change Requests and Work Performance Reports into the Perform Integrated Change Control process. What problems would the project have if the work on that arrow was neglected?

4.6 Perform Integrated Change Control
Understand the Basics First

Write the ITTO's for the process **Perform Integrated Change Control** below:

Inputs	Tools & Techniques	Outputs
1.	1.	1.
2.	2.	2.
3.	3.	3.
4.	4.	
5.	5.	
6.		

In the space below. For each ITTO, if the item listed is a generic category, list at least one example that could be included:

Integrated Change Control - The Project Management knowledge areas are generally managed in an integrated manner with an understanding that a change in one area can impact any or all of the other knowledge areas. There are three basic considerations of a change control process and plan:

1. Consider the impact of the change before implementing the change. Changes should be beneficial or necessary or associated with a compliance directive and agreed upon by a decision-making group. The decision-making group is generally referred to as the CCB or Change Control Board.
2. Determine that a change has occurred by comparing the baseline plans with actual results. A baseline will provide the ability to clearly define changes in or slippages in project schedules or budget overruns and other deviations from the plan.
3. Determine when to make a change and how to introduce the change in a way that will minimize impact to project execution or to an organization's ongoing operations.

Change Control Board (CCB) – A team or group of stakeholders designated or empowered to review and determine the value of a change and to approve or deny change requests.

Configuration Management – A process that will ensure that configuration changes (changes to features, functions, physical characteristics of a product) are managed and approved to prevent or reduce the risks of additional cost, scope changes, or other effects on the project.

<u>Become Better Prepared by Practicing This</u>

Study Figure 4-13. Perform Integrated Change Control Data Flow Diagram on p. 114 of the *PMBOK Guide*.

- Mark where each of the outputs falls in the flow, with special attention paid to what process that output flows into.
- Notice that there are change requests and then there are approved change requests.
- Notice where the change log flows.

5.5 Validate Scope
<u>Understand the Basics First</u>

Write the ITTO's for the process **Validate Scope** below:

Inputs	Tools & Techniques	Outputs
1.	1.	1.
2.	2.	2.
3.		3.
4.		4.

In the space below. For each ITTO, if the item listed is a generic category, list at least one example that could be included:

Validating the scope ensures what is produced during project execution is what was intended to be produced. The goal is to achieve acceptance of deliverables. Scope verification is a check to see that the right work is being done and the correct outputs are being produced. Verification is accomplished when the customer or receiver of the output formally approves the result. This is known as formal acceptance.

Become Better Prepared by Practicing This

Study Figure 5-16. Validate Scope Data Flow Diagram on p. 164 of the PMBOK.

- Notice that Verified deliverables flows out of Control Quality
- Notice that accepted deliverable flow into Close Project or Phase
- What happens to unaccepted deliverables in this flow?

5.6 Control Scope

Understand the Basics First

Write the ITTO's for the process **Control Scope** below:

Inputs	Tools & Techniques	Outputs
1.	1.	1.
2.		2.
3.		3.
4.		4.

In the space below. For each ITTO, if the item listed is a generic category, list at least one example that could be included:

Control Scope – Manage changes to the scope of the project to avoid unauthorized changes and scope creep. A change control process is established during the early stages of the project and enforced throughout the project life cycle.

6.6 Control Schedule

<u>Understand the Basics First</u>

Write the ITTO's for the process **Control Schedule** below:

Inputs	Tools & Techniques	Outputs
1.	1.	1.
2.	2.	2.
3.	3.	3.
4.	4.	4.
	5.	5.
	6.	
	7.	

In the space below. For each ITTO, if the item listed is a generic category, list at least one example that could be included:

Control Schedule: Review of project progress reports, project performance, change requests, and variance analysis. Utilize a change control system and take the appropriate corrective action. Document your schedule lessons learned.

Schedule Compression Techniques

Fast Tracking – Overlapping of activities normally done in series. Risk must be considered when using the fast tracking technique.

Crashing – Adding resources, using overtime. This method usually increases overall cost of the activities and possibly the project. Crashing is focused on the critical path and the least cost that may be expended to achieve the desired result.

Become Better by Practicing This

Build a network diagram based on the project information below. Then answer the series of questions that follow.

Activity Name	Preceding Activity (Assume all are finish-to-start relationships)	Time (weeks)	Planned Value	Assigned Team
A	-	7	$1,000	Fred
B	-	8	$22,000	Mary
C	-	6	$3,000	Jane & Team
D	A	6	$5,000	Fred
E	B	6	$11,000	Mary
F	B	8	$1,000	Jane & Team
G	C	4	$5,000	Jane & Team
H	D, E	7	$10,000	Fred
I	F, G, H	3	$1,000	Jane & Team
J	I	3	$5,000	Fred
K	I	2	$1,000	Mary
L	I	5	$10,000	Jane & Team

Start by Drawing Your Network Diagram:

1. What activities create the project's critical path?

2. What is G's slack time if C used 6 weeks of its available slack time?

3. During week 1, what activity is your greatest concern?

4. If Jane and her Team can't do any work on this project during weeks 9 and 10, can we still work with them and achieve our schedule?

5. If you had to pick 4 milestone points in the project based on the network diagram, where would they fall?

6. Assume you are the project manager and you want to take a 2-week vacation sometime during the project. When is the best time for you to be out on vacation? Does the network diagram or Gantt chart do a better job of helping you make this decision?

7. Create a line chart of the cumulative planned project expenditures assuming work happens as soon as possible, and that billing is done upon completion of the activities.

8. Compare and contrast the usefulness of the network diagram, Gantt chart, and line chart of expenditures.

9. If the customer wants the project schedule shortened, what is the best activity to focus on shortening (crashing)? The second and third best? Remember that it only pays to crash the work that is on the critical path because the other work has float/slack time available. What are the best crash decisions if crashing had no additional cost?

10. Assuming the crash table information in the table that follows to be correct, what are the best crash priorities based purely on cost?

Do These Steps to Fully Prepare

Determine what task you would pay to crash first, based on prioritizing the cheapest first and continuing to at least the third priority point. Keep the critical path in mind, because paying to crash a task that is not on the critical path would not help.

Crash Table

Task	Current		Compressed		Weekly cost to compress (crash cost)	Crash priority
	Duration	Cost	Duration	Cost		
A	7	$1,000	3	$5,000		
B	8	$22,000	4	$30,000		
C	6	$3,000	5	$4,000		
D	6	$5,000	6	$5,000		
E	6	$11,000	4	$17,000		
F	8	$1,000	7	$2,000		
G	4	$5,000	2	$8,000		
H	7	$10,000	3	$25,000		
I	3	$1,000	2	$2,000		
J	3	$5,000	2	$6,000		
K	2	$1,000	1	$1,500		
L	5	$10,000	2	$16,000		

7.4 Control Cost

Understand the Basics First

Write the ITTO's for the process **Control Cost** below:

Inputs	Tools & Techniques	Outputs
1.	1.	1.
2.	2.	2.
3.	3.	3.
4.	4.	4.
5.		5.

In the space below. For each ITTO, if the item listed is a generic category, list at least one example that could be included:

Control Cost – Managing change requests through a cost change control system. Cost control includes the use of performance data to identify variances. Cost control also includes project reviews, variance management, and project performance reviews. Earned value management is used to identify variances and trends.

Review the following Earned Value acronyms and formulas:

CV = EV - AC	Positive is GOOD. Negative is BAD.
CPI = EV / AC	CPI of 1 means exactly on budget. Less than 1 means over budget (poor efficiency in the management of budget) Greater than 1 means under budget or high efficiency in the use of funds.
SV = EV - PV	Positive is GOOD. Negative is BAD.
SPI = EV / PV	SPI of 1 means exactly on schedule. A SPI that is greater than 1 means better performance than plan. A SPI that is less than 1 means the project is not performing as well as originally planned.
ETC = EAC - AC	The Estimate to Complete is the <u>remaining</u> amount of funds estimated to be needed from the reporting date to the end.
Percent Complete = EV / BAC * 100	
VAC = BAC - EAC	
EV = % complete * BAC	
% SPENT = AC / BAC x 100	

<u>Become Better Prepared by Practicing This</u>

Simple Earned Value Formula Memory Technique

Below is a memory technique to help you remember the Earned Value (EV) formulas. Start writing down your EV formulas by putting these things in a vertical column on your sheet:

    SV

    SPI

    CV

    CPI

Then add the equals sign to each row, so it looks like this:

    SV=

    SPI=

    CV=

    CPI=

Then add the EV part of the equation to each row, so it looks like this:

    SV=EV

    SPI=EV

    CV=EV

    CPI=EV

Then in the last step you have to remember a bit about what each thing is, but the previous steps got the logic all set up for you to complete the formulas based on what the relative information is. There are two divide formulas and two subtraction formulas. The indexes use the divide formulas. That goes as follows:

    SV=EV-PV

    SPI=EV/PV

    CV=EV-AC

    CPI=EV/AC

Remember, for variance, subtract from EV. For an index, divide EV by something. For cost-related formulas, use AC. For schedule-related formulas, use PV.

Earned Value Drill

Complete the chart below.

BCWP (EV)	BCWS (PV)	ACWP (AC)	AHEAD OF SCHEDULE	BEHIND SCHEDULE	COST UNDERRUN	COST OVERRUN
7000	9000	7000		-2000	0	0
7000	6000	5000	1000		2000	
3000	3000	6000	0	0		-3000
5000	7000	6000		-2000		-1000
7000	8000	7000		-1000	0	0
9000	6000	8000	3000		1000	
4000	3000	5000	1000			-1000
6000	7000	5000		-1000	1000	
2000	3000	4000		-1000		-2000
8000	6000	6000	2000		2000	
7000	9000	9000		-2000		-2000
5000	5000	8000	0	0		-3000
5000	4000	3000	1000		2000	
9000	7000	8000	2000		1000	
5000	5000	5000	0	0	0	0
8000	9000	7000		-1000	1000	
5000	4000	6000	1000			-1000
9000	7000	7000	2000		2000	
1000	2000	2000		-1000		-1000

Do These Steps to Fully Prepare

Write down the four simple EV formulas for SV, SPI, CV, and CPI:

8.3 Control Quality
Understand the Basics First

Write the ITTO's for the process **Control Quality** below:

Inputs	Tools & Techniques	Outputs
1.	1.	1.
2.	2.	2.
3.	3.	3.
4.	4.	4.
5.	5.	5.
6.	6.	6.
7.		

In the space below. For each ITTO, if the item listed is a generic category, list at least one example that could be included:

Sampling:

- Attribute sampling is a pass or fail approach with no flexibility.
- Variable sampling allows for some tolerance and is measured using a specific scale with identified and acceptable variances.

Inspection – May include management walk through, testing, and reviews.

Control Charts – Rule of 7 / 21 (7 points needed to determine a trend or run, 21 points for the sampling to be statistically valid).

Control charts are used to determine if a process is in control or out of control. Observe data points within the upper and lower control limits of the control chart. Items requiring attention are trends, runs, patterns, and data points that fall outside of the upper or lower control limit. A process is "in control" when the data points are distributed evenly above and below the process centerline or average with no trends, runs, patterns or other conditions that may lead to an assignable cause.

Pareto Analysis – 80 / 20 rule (80% of problems are associated with 20% of causes). Data is presented as a histogram and ranked by frequency of occurrence.

Cause and Effect Diagrams – Also known as Fishbone diagrams or Ishikawa diagram (generally used to determine root cause).

Other Diagramming Methods include:

- Flow charting
- Histograms
- Run Charts
- Scatter Diagrams – Graphs pairs of numerical data, with one variable on each axis, to look for a relationship (correlation) between them.

Remember to document **lessons learned** at the completion of the quality control process.

9.6 Control Resources

Understand the Basics First

Write the ITTO's for the process **Control Resources** below:

Inputs	Tools & Techniques	Outputs
1.	1.	1.
2.	2.	2.
3.	3.	3.
4.	4.	4.
5.		

In the space below. For each ITTO, if the item listed is a generic category, list at least one example that could be included:

Control Resources: Ensuring that the physical resources assigned and allocated to the project are available as planned, as well as monitoring the planned versus actual utilization of resources and taking corrective action as necessary.

Become Better by Practicing This

Discuss how the Project Management Information System can be beneficial in this process.

10.3 Monitor Communications

Understand the Basics First

Write the ITTO's for the process **Monitor Communications** below:

Inputs	Tools & Techniques	Outputs
1.	1.	1.
2.	2.	2.
3.	3.	3.
4.	4.	4.
5.	5.	

In the space below. For each ITTO, if the item listed is a generic category, list at least one example that could be included:

11.7 Monitor Risks

Understand the Basics First

Write the ITTO's for the process **Monitor Risks** below:

Inputs	Tools & Techniques	Outputs
1.	1.	1.
2.	2.	2.
3.	3.	3.
4.		4.
		5.

In the space below. For each ITTO, if the item listed is a generic category, list at least one example that could be included:

Risk Assessment – Identification of new risks, reassessment of current and previously identified risks, closing of risks.

Risk Audits – Examining the effectiveness of risk responses.

Variance and Trend Analysis – Comparing actual results to planned results.

Reserve Analysis – Effect of risk responses on the reserves that have been planned. Determining if the remaining reserves are adequate.

12.3 Control Procurements

Understand the Basics First

Write the ITTO's for the process **Control Procurements** below:

Inputs	Tools & Techniques	Outputs
1.	1.	1.
2.	2.	2.
3.	3.	3.
4.	4.	4.
5.	5.	5.
6.		6.
7.		7.
8.		

In the space below. For each ITTO, if the item listed is a generic category, list at least one example that could be included:

Define these terms in your own words:

Contract change control system _____

Procurement performance reviews _____

Inspections and audits _____

Performance reporting _____

Payment systems _____

Claims administration _____

Records management system _____

13.4 Monitor Stakeholder Engagement

Understand the Basics First

Inputs	Tools & Techniques	Outputs
1.	1.	1.
2.	2.	2.
3.	3.	3.
4.	4.	4.
5.	5.	
	6.	

In the space below. For each ITTO, if the item listed is a generic category, list at least one example that could be included:

Become Better by Practicing This

Think about these aspects of your project:

1. How active is your project sponsor? And, how does this impact your project?

2. Are you making your issues log visible and are you getting adequate involvements from your sponsors in addressing the project issues?

3. Are you getting the best advice out of your subject matter experts?

4. Are your project team member's levels of engagement high?

Section 12: Closing Process Group

CLOSING PROCESS GROUP

4.7 Close Project or Phase

<u>Understand the Basics First</u>

Inputs	Tools & Techniques	Outputs
1.	1.	1.
2.	2.	2.
3.	3.	3.
4.		4.
5.		
6.		
7.		
8.		

In the space below. For each ITTO, if the item listed is a generic category, list at least one example that could be included:

Project Manager Role - Research shows that few project managers have the authority to formally and legally close a contract. Project managers are responsible to determine that work is complete, records are indexed and archived, and responsibilities are transferred appropriately.

Section 13: Final Preparation for Your Exam

Terminology Review

Although the terms listed below are not all of those you should know, they are a good review.

Constraints and Assumptions – Constraints are limitations that have been imposed such as budget caps, predetermined milestones or project end dates. Constraints are also associated with imposed dates such as must start no later than, must finish no later than. Constraints may also be associated with contractual agreements. Constraints are not considered boundaries. Project boundaries are generally those items that have been agreed upon between the buyer and seller regarding what the project scope of work is and what it will not include. During contract negotiations the boundaries are established regarding what work will be done and what work is excluded from the project. *Assumption*s are commonly used for planning purposes. The definition of an assumption is: an item you can believe to be true, real, or certain for planning purposes. Assumptions are not grounded in fact and should be validated.

Work Performance Information – This information is used for reporting project status. Performance information includes: schedule progress, status of deliverables, costs incurred, quality assessments, completion of deliverables, and the achievement of a milestone.

Configuration Management – Concerned with managing changes to the features, functions, and physical characteristics of the deliverable of the project over time. This often pertains to the product of a project. An example may be a specific function in a software application. The function is given an identification number and as the function's requirements and specifications change over time, the identification number stays the same even if it is renamed. The configuration management system will help answer the question regarding what date its attributes changed. Ideally it would help answer questions regarding what features it had at any prior specific time.

Interviews – Direct discussions, informal or formal, with stakeholders.

Focus Groups – These are carefully planned group discussions conducted by trained moderators. The purpose is to learn more about the expectations of the stakeholders. A small number of questions developed in advance are used to generate in-depth consideration of a narrowly defined topic. Focus groups examine perceptions, feelings, attitudes and ideas.

Facilitated Workshops – Defining requirements in focused sessions with stakeholders from several functional groups.

Group Creativity Techniques:

Brainstorming – Rapid generation of ideas

Nominal Group Technique – Combination of brainstorming and using a voting system to prioritize the items identified during brainstorming. The voting is done anonymously to minimize influence from other stakeholders. The nominal group technique (NGT) is a decision-making method for use among groups of many sizes, who want to make their decision quickly, as by a vote, but want everyone's opinions taken into account. Each person evaluates the ideas and individually and anonymously votes for the best ideas.

Delphi Technique – Use of subject matter experts who remain anonymous to each other.

Idea/Mind Mapping – A mind map is a diagram used to represent words, ideas, tasks, or other items linked to and arranged around a central key word or idea. Mind maps are used to generate, visualize, structure, and classify ideas, and as an aid to studying and organizing information, solving problems, making decisions, and writing.

Affinity Diagram - This tool is commonly used within project management and allows large numbers of ideas stemming from brainstorming to be sorted into groups for review and analysis.

Group Decision Making Techniques – Unanimity: agreement by everyone. Majority: Agreement by more than 50% of a group. Plurality: Decision is based on the largest block within a group, but the block is less than 50% of the group. Dictatorship/Autocratic: No discussion.

Observations – Example: Use cases. Watching a process to gather information.

Prototypes – Tangible, working models that help to provide feedback.

Scope Control includes the scope change control system, variance analysis, re- planning and configuration management. A change control system is necessary to make sure that unauthorized changes are not implemented and to prevent scope creep.

Review Formulas and Other Cost and Financial Terminology

Project Selection – Economic Models and terms include the following:

Return on Investment (ROI) - The average returns of the project divided by the average investment in the project.

ROI = (average returns / Average Costs) x 100%.

Example: The cumulative net cash flows of the project are expected to be $11.9 million for the 5 years of the project. The average net cash flow will be 11.9 / 5 = $2.38 million. The company will invest an average of $5.3 million each year.

ROI = 2.38 / 5.3 = 45%

Break-Even Analysis – Determines the point where the outgoing cash flow and incoming cash flow are equal.

Present Value – Determines the current or present value of a future investment. The time value of money is considered. $PV = FV / (1+r)^n$

Future Value $FV = PV (1+r)^n$

Net Present Value (NPV) – Sum up the present value of each year of the investment then subtract the initial investment. A positive NPV indicates a profitable project.

NPV (Net Present Value) = $FV/(1+r)^n$

- FV = Future Value, r= interest rate, n= no. of time periods
- Higher NPV is better

Internal Rate of Return (IRR) is the average annual return earned through the life of an investment. Calculating it requires iterations to determine at what rate the Net Present Value (NPV) will become zero. Compare the calculated IRR rate with Hurdle Rate (the minimum acceptable rate of return). The higher the IRR the better the investment.

Payback Period – It determines the amount of time required to recover the initial investment. A shorter payback period is better. This technique does not consider the time value of money.

Example: The total cost of an information system is estimated to be $100,000. The yearly benefits are estimated to be $25,000. The payback period is 100,000 / 25,000 = 4 years.

Sunk Cost – Funds already spent. Sunk costs are generally not considered when making decisions about moving forward with a project during a phase review.

Indirect Costs vs. Direct Costs – Labor and material are considered direct costs to the project. Indirect costs may be associated with benefits and the costs of maintaining a building such as rent, electric power, or office support.

Benefit to Cost Ratio (BCR) - The benefits of an investment (at present value) divided by the cost of the investment (at present value).

B/C = Present value of revenues / present value of costs

Example: If the present value of revenues = $80,691 and the present value of costs = $51,265 then B/C = 80,691 / 51,265 = 1.57

B/C greater than (1) indicates that benefits are greater than the costs and the project is favorable.

Earned Value Formulas to remember:

    EV - AC = Cost Variance CV (negative cost variance =overrun)
    EV - PV = Schedule Variance SV (negative means behind schedule)
    EV / AC = Cost Performance Index (efficiency in the mgt. of costs)
    EV / PV = Schedule performance index (efficiency in schedule performance)

Performance Index – If the PI is equal to 1 this means there is no variance, or the project is on plan. IF the PI is greater than 1 it means better performance than plan. If the PI is less than 1 it means the project is not performing as well as originally planned.

The Week and Day before Your Exam

One Week Before the Exam

Practice Your Brain Dump Sheet
During the test you may become mentally fatigued and find it difficult to remember certain concepts. By this time, you should have a good idea of the topics that you find challenging. For many people it is the Earned Value Formulas. Some people struggle with differentiating two terms (e.g.: qualitative versus quantitative). Whatever these topics are for you, they should be noted on your brain dump sheet to help you as you proceed through your test. Practice making this dump sheet and learn to use it during your practice Exams.

Review All Formulas
Review and practice all formulas to ensure that you remember each one and its application.

Take Practice Exams
Taking practice exams is the best way to determine how ready you are to pass the exam. It is recommended that you not only take practice exams, but that you analyze the results to create your study punch list. You will find many example questions and exams on the internet.

PMP Practice Exams

Exam Tracking Log

Track your PMP® practice exam confidence level. From this you should make a list of the topics that tend to have low confidence, indicating what you need to study further.

Practice #1:

Exam Source: _____

Date:

#	Topic	90%	50%	25%	No Clue
1					
2					
3					
4					
5					
6					
7					
8					
9					
10					
11					
12					
13					
14					
15					
16					
17					
18					
19					
20					
21					
22					
23					
24					
25					
26					
27					
28					
29					
30					
31					
32					
33					

34					
35					
36					
37					
38					
39					
40					
41					
42					
43					
44					
45					
46					
47					
48					
49					
50					
51					
52					
53					
54					
55					
56					
57					
58					
59					
60					
61					
62					
63					
64					
65					
66					
67					
68					
69					
70					
71					
72					
73					
74					
75					
76					
77					

78					
79					
80					
81					
82					
83					
84					
85					
86					
87					
88					
89					
90					
91					
92					
93					
94					
95					
96					
97					
98					
99					
100					
101					
102					
103					
104					
105					
106					
107					
108					
109					
110					
111					
112					
113					
114					
115					
116					
117					
118					
119					
120					
121					

#					
122					
123					
124					
125					
126					
127					
128					
129					
130					
131					
132					
133					
134					
135					
136					
137					
138					
139					
140					
141					
142					
143					
144					
145					
146					
147					
148					
149					
150					
151					
152					
153					
154					
155					
156					
157					
158					
159					
160					
161					
162					
163					
164					
165					

166					
167					
168					
169					
170					
171					
172					
1173					
174					
175					
176					
177					
178					
179					
180					
181					
182					
183					
184					
185					
186					
187					
188					
189					
190					
191					
192					
193					
194					
195					
196					
197					
198					
199					
200					
201					
202					
203					
204					
205					
206					
207					
208					
209					

210				
211				
212				
213				
214				
215				
216				
217				
218				
219				
220				
221				
222				
223				
224				
225				
226				
227				
228				
229				
230				
231				
232				
233				
234				
235				
236				
237				
238				
239				
240				
241				
242				
243				
244				
245				
246				
247				
248				
249				
250				
251				
252				
253				

254					
255					
256					
257					
258					
259					
260					
261					
262					
263					
264					
265					
266					
267					
268					
269					
270					
271					
272					
273					
274					
275					
276					
277					
278					
279					
280					
281					
282					
283					
284					
285					
286					
287					
288					
289					
290					
291					
292					
293					
294					
295					
296					
297					

298					
299					
300					
301					
302					
303					
304					
305					
306					
307					
308					
309					
310					
311					
312					
313					
314					
315					
316					
317					
318					
319					
320					
321					
322					
323					
324					
325					
326					
327					
328					
329					
330					
331					
332					
333					
334					
335					
336					
337					
338					
339					
340					
341					

342					
343					
344					
345					
346					
347					
348					
349					
350					
351					
352					
353					
354					
355					
356					
357					
358					
359					
360					
361					
362					
363					
364					
365					
366					
367					
368					
369					
370					
371					
372					
373					
374					
375					
376					
377					
378					
379					
380					
381					
382					
383					
384					
385					

386					
387					
388					
389					
390					
391					
392					
393					
394					
395					
396					
397					
398					
399					
400					

The Day Before the Exam

Take a break from study and allow yourself to rest. At this point you should be ready to go. Verify the location of the exam and obtain directions as necessary. Prepare the items you need: your picture ID and a second form of identification. Remember, you will not be allowed to carry any personal items such as smart phones, pens, or any other items into the test area.

Get some exercise and get a good night's sleep the evening before you take the exam.

At the Exam

1. Make sure your entry into the exam center goes smoothly by remembering these things:
   - Take your photo ID
   - Plan not to take anything into the exam with you. You will have to leave your watch, cell phone, and any other valuables outside the testing room.
5. Eat a normal size healthy meal and try to stick with your normal amount of caffeine. This is not a time to try a new food or eliminate or increase any influencing factors such as caffeine.
6. Upon Entering the Exam Room
   6.1 Take 5 – 10 minutes to create your brain dump sheet.
   6.2 Remember the strategy of flagging questions that you can't figure out.
7. Before hitting the submit button
   7.1 **Make sure that you have left no questions unanswered.** Even if you don't know the answer, you should guess. You have no chance of getting credit for an unanswered question and you have a 25% chance if you totally guess. Your odds are even better if you can eliminate even one of the wrong answers.
   7.2 Hit the submit button.
   7.3 Your exam results will quickly display on the screen.

After the Exam

1. Celebrate!
2. Notify those who helped you along the way.
3. After passing, you are allowed to put PMP® after your name immediately.
4. Record your new credential in your professional credentials, including such places as your LinkedIn profile (which has a section for credentials).
5. Your PMP® credential renewal process, discussed earlier, begins immediately. You have 3 years to earn 60 PDUs after passing the exam. But as long as you stay current with the PDU reporting, you will not need to reapply or take the test again.

Answer Key

Section 3: PMBOK Framework and Foundations

Project Definition
1. Timeframe has a definite beginning and end
2. Project team is temporary
3. It creates a product
4. It is one of a kind
5. It has specific and measurable results
6. It has allocated resources

Project Management Definition
The PMBOK sixth edition glossary defines Project Management as the application of knowledge, skill, tools, and techniques to project activities to meet project requirements.

Other definitions:

Project management is the practice of initiating, planning, executing, controlling, and closing the work of a team to achieve specific goals and meet specific success criteria at the specified time. (Wikipedia.com)

Project management is the application of processes, methods, knowledge, skills and experience to achieve the project objectives. (APM.org.uk)

Organizational Structures

	Functional	Weak Matrix	Balanced Matrix	Strong Matrix	Project Oriented
Authority	PM has little to no authority	PM has low level of authority	PM has moderate or equal authority	PM has greater authority	PM has high level of authority
Advantages	Clearly defined career paths, team members report to one supervisor, Similar resources are centralized	Someone assigned to focus on project objectives (coordinator), team member maintains "home"	Strong PM control, reports into a PMO, team member maintains "home"	Loyalty to the project, more effective project communications, resources dedicated to project tasks	PM has full authority, teams report to PM, adaptive, co-located teams when possible, better communication
Disadvantages	People place more emphasis on their functional area expertise vs Project; PM has little authority. No Career path in PM	PM has little authority and reports to functional manager; Power resides within functional area	Potential for conflict, differing priorities between functional area and project	No "home" when current project is done, duplication in job functionality across projects, less efficient use of resources.	Abundance of power can be an issue, insecurity of team members as they disband when project complete, duplication of effort

Project Stakeholders

An individual, group or organization that may affect, be affected by, or perceive itself to be affected by a decision, activity, or outcome of a project, program, or portfolio.

They are typically the members of a project team, project managers, executives, project sponsors, customers, and users.

Project Governance
The framework, functions, and processes that guide project management activities in order to create a unique product, service or result to meet organizational, strategic, and operational goals. EX: Rules, Norms, Policies, Escalation Procedures.

Project Life Cycles
1. Predictive
2. Agile
3. Iterative
4. Incremental
5. Hybrid

Difference between Standards and Regulations
Regulations are requirements imposed by a governmental body whereas Standards are documents that are established by an authority, custom or general consent as a model or example. Conformance with a standard is voluntary, conformance is mandatory with a Regulation. EX: Regulations around speed limits, vs. the PMBOK is a standard.

Organizational Influences
Organizational culture can impact project success in many ways including: attitude toward conformance to following procedures, organizational views toward importance of training, a culture that supports projects as important to success. If your organization supports, or emphasizes their importance, the results will be more successful than if these things are not fully supported. Organizational structure can impact the level of importance placed on project vs ongoing operations or the ability to get resources for your project, or who has the authority over the resources on a project.

EEF examples:

organizational culture, structure and governance, existing facilities or equipment, software tools, approved providers and subcontractors, existing resources expertise, marketplace conditions, legal restrictions, industry standards, weather

OPA examples:

processes, policies, procedures, organization knowledge base, templates

Distinguishing between EEFs and OPAs

EEF	**OPA**	Stakeholder register templates (*PMBOK® Guide* p. 510)
EEF	OPA	Organizational culture and structure (*PMBOK® Guide* p. 510)
EEF	**OPA**	Lessons learned from previous projects or phases (*PMBOK® Guide* p. 510)
EEF	OPA	Governmental or industry standards (*PMBOK® Guide* p. 510)
EEF	OPA	Product standards (*PMBOK® Guide* p. 510)
EEF	**OPA**	Stakeholder registers from previous projects (*PMBOK® Guide* p. 510)
EEF	OPA	Global trends (*PMBOK® Guide* p. 510)
EEF	OPA	Regional practices (*PMBOK® Guide* p. 510)
EEF	OPA	Local habits (*PMBOK® Guide* p. 510)
EEF	OPA	Political climate (*PMBOK® Guide* p. 519)
EEF	**OPA**	Organizational communication requirements (*PMBOK® Guide* p. 520)
EEF	**OPA**	Stakeholder notifications (*PMBOK® Guide* p. 526)
EEF	**OPA**	Issue management procedures (*PMBOK® Guide* p. 526)
EEF	**OPA**	Project reports (*PMBOK® Guide* p. 388)
EEF	**OPA**	Project presentations (*PMBOK® Guide* p. 388)
EEF	**OPA**	Organizational Risk Policy (*PMBOK® Guide* p. 403)
EEF	**OPA**	Change Control procedures (*PMBOK® Guide* p. 530)
EEF	**OPA**	Feedback from stakeholders (*PMBOK® Guide* p. 520)

Section 4: Knowledge Areas and Process Groups

Understand the Basics First

Total Processes = 49

See Table 1-4 page 25: Project Management Process Group and Knowledge Area Mapping

Process Groups

Initiating (2)
Planning (24)
Executing (10)
Monitoring and Controlling (12)
Closing (1)

Knowledge Areas

Project Integration Management (7)
Project Scope Management (6)
Project Schedule Management (6)
Project Cost Management (4)
Project Quality Management (3)
Project Resources Management (6)
Project Communications Management (3)
Project Risk Management (7)
Project Procurement Management (3)
Project Stakeholder Management (4)

Process Names
Become Better Prepared by Practicing This

See Table 1-4 page 25 of the PMBOK: Project Management Process Group and Knowledge Area Mapping

Project Management Knowledge Areas

Integration Management (PMBOK Chapter 4)
1. Examples of balancing competing demands:
   a. Triple constraint 1: Time, Cost, Scope (or quality). You can pick two, but the third will have to be adjusted.
   b. Triple constraint 2: Resources, Financials and Stakeholders. Once again you can pick two, but the third will have to be adjusted.
2. What are the 7 Integration processes?

	Initiating	Planning	Executing	Monitoring & Controlling	Closing
Integration	4.1 Develop Project Charter	4.2 Develop Project Management Plan	4.3 Direct and Manage Project Work 4.4 Manage Project Knowledge	4.5 Monitor and Control Project Work 4.6 Perform Integrated Change Control	4.7 Close Project or Phase

Scope Management (PMBOK Chapter 5)
1. What are the 6 Scope processes?

	Initiating	Planning	Executing	Monitoring & Controlling	Closing
Scope		5.1 Plan Scope Management 5.2 Collect Requirements 5.3 Define Scope 5.4 Create WBS		5.5 Validate Scope 5.6 Control Scope	

2. How a WBS helps the project team
   - helps team understand their commitment.
   - allows the team members to fully understand the what, when, why and how of the desired results at each phase of the project.

3. Requirements are specified and stated needs; expectations are unspecified/ unstated needs. We differentiate between them because a requirement can be used to determine if the deliverable is complete - it's quantifiable, something you can confirm through inspection. HOWEVER - needs and expectations are perceptions, which if not managed, will diminish stakeholder satisfaction (and potentially create a project failure).

4. The scope baseline is the approved detailed project scope statement and its associated WBS and WBS dictionary. It acts as the reference point through the project's life.

Schedule Management (PMBOK Chapter 6)

1. Critical Path: The series of tasks that must finish on time for the entire project to finish on schedule. It is the longest path through the network.
2. Fast tracking - A schedule compression technique in which activities or phases normally done in sequence are performed in parallel for at least a portion of their duration.
3. Crashing - A technique used to shorten the schedule duration for the least incremental cost by adding resources.
4. What are the 6 schedule management processes?

	Initiating	Planning	Executing	Monitoring & Controlling	Closing
Schedule		6.1 Plan Schedule Management 6.2 Define Activities 6.3 Sequence Activities 6.4 Estimate Activity Durations 6.5 Develop Schedule		6.6 Control Schedule	

Cost Management (PMBOK Chapter 7)

1. What method of status reporting does the PMBOK promote for measuring cost variances? Earned Value Management helps project managers monitor project performance based on work performed vs. work planned.

2. What are the 4 cost management processes?

	Initiating	Planning	Executing	Monitoring & Controlling	Closing
Cost		7.1 Plan Cost Management 7.2 Estimate Costs 7.3 Determine Budget		7.4 Control Cost	

Quality Management (PMBOK Chapter 8)

1. What are the 3 quality processes?

	Initiating	Planning	Executing	Monitoring & Controlling	Closing
Quality		8.1 Plan Quality Management	8.2 Manage Quality	8.3 Control Quality	

2. **PDCA** (plan–do–check–act or plan–do–check–adjust)
3. Key concepts for project quality management
   1. Failure to meet quality requirements can have serious negative consequences for any or all of the stakeholders.
   2. Quality and grade are not the same concepts.
   3. Prevention over Inspection.

4. Cost of quality. Refers to all of the costs that are incurred over the life of the product or service by investment in preventing nonconformance to requirements, appraisal of the product or service for conformance to requirements, and failure to meet requirements.
5. Five levels of increasingly effective quality management are:
    a. Most expensive approach is customer finds the defects.
    b. Detect and correct defects before sent to the customer.
    c. Use quality assurance to examine and correct the process.
    d. Incorporate quality into the planning and designing of the product.
    e. Create a culture that is committed to quality.
4. The Malcolm Baldrige Quality process and award – is an award established by the U.S. Congress in 1987 to raise awareness of quality management and recognize U.S. companies that have implemented successful quality management systems. Awards can be given annually in six categories: manufacturing, service, small business, education, healthcare and nonprofit. The award is named after the late Secretary of Commerce Malcolm Baldrige, a proponent of quality management. The U.S. Commerce Department's National Institute of Standards and Technology manages the award, and ASQ administers it.
5. ISO compatibility means: Compatible with the International Standards Organization (ISO) standards.

Resource Management (PMBOK Chapter 9)
1. What are the 6 resource management processes?

	Initiating	Planning	Executing	Monitoring & Controlling	Closing
Resource		9.1 Plan Resource Management 9.2 Estimate Activity Resources	9.3 Acquire Resources 9.4 Develop Team 9.5 Manage Team	9.6 Control Resources	

Communications Management (PMBOK Chapter 10)
1. It is commonly stated that **90 percent** of a project manager's time is spent communicating.
2. What are the 3 communication processes?

	Initiating	Planning	Executing	Monitoring & Controlling	Closing
Communications		10.1 Plan Communications Management	10.2 Manage Communications	10.3 Monitor Communications	

Risk Management (PMBOK Chapter 11)

1. What are the 7 risk processes?

	Initiating	Planning	Executing	Monitoring & Controlling	Closing
Risk		11.1 Plan Risk Management 11.2 Identify Risks 11.3 Perform Qualitative Risk Analysis 11.4 Perform Quantitative Risk Analysis 11.5 Plan Risk Responses	11.6 Implement Risk Responses	11.7 Monitor Risks	

2. What are the 5 positive risk responses?
    1. *Escalate*
    2. *Enhance*
    3. *Exploit*
    4. *Accept*
    5. *Share*

3. What are the 5 risk negative responses?
    1. *Escalate*
    2. *Mitigate*
    3. *Transfer*
    4. *Avoid*
    5. *Accept*

Procurement Management (PMBOK Chapter 12)

1. Procurement involves both materials and services.
2. What are the 3 procurement processes?

	Initiating	Planning	Executing	Monitoring & Controlling	Closing
Procurement		12.1 Plan Procurement Management	12.2 Conduct Procurements	12.3 Control Procurements	

Stakeholder Management (PMBOK Chapter 13)

1. What are the 4 stakeholder processes?

	Initiating	Planning	Executing	Monitoring & Controlling	Closing
Stakeholder	13.1 Identify Stakeholders	13.2 Plan Stakeholder Engagement	13.3 Manage Stakeholder Engagement	13.4 Monitor Stakeholder Engagement	

2. Stakeholder Identification should start as early as possible during the Initiating process but will continue throughout the project.

Section 5: Project Selection and Project Initiating Process Group

PROJECT SELECTION

Define these in your own words:

Time value of money: a dollar in your hand today is worth more than a dollar you will receive in the future because a dollar in hand today can be invested to turn into more money in the future.

Opportunity Cost: refers to the value forgone in order to make one particular investment instead of another.

Sunk Cost: is a cost that has already been incurred and cannot be recovered.

Net Present Value (NPV) Sample Problem

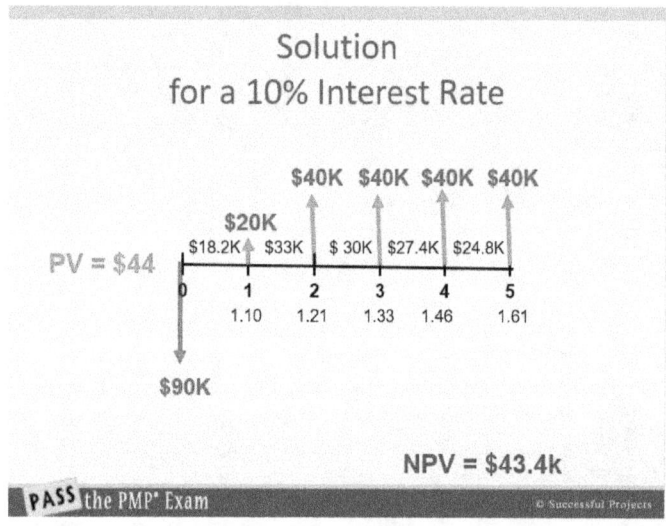

Let's use our visual timeline to build our answer. Start by drawing out 5 years on a timeline and indicate the $90K investment at the beginning. Then indicate the savings, above the line. We have the planned cost savings of $20K at the end of year one, and $40K at the end of each of the following years.

Then, let's add the interest, or time effect, to these forecasted savings. If the interest rate is 10% per year, it doesn't affect our initial investment of $90K. But after time starts passing, we calculate each year's effect by the number of the year plus the interest rate to the power of the number of years. For year 1 that factor is 1.1, for year 2 it is 1.21, for year 3 it is 1.33, year 4 it is 1.46, and for year 5 it is 1.61.

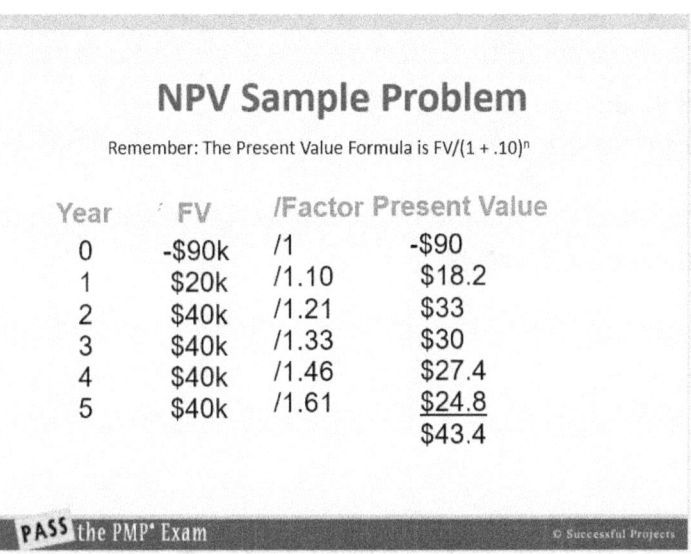

We subtract the $90K and add the income for each year based on the savings divided by the Interest Factor, giving us the present value for the savings each year, which nets out at $43.4K.

Assuming the cost of money is 10%, what would the NPV of this project be? NPV = 43.4K

Payback Period Sample Problem:

Payback period = $50k/$35k = 1.43 yrs

Benefit / Cost Ratio Sample Problem:

Benefit / Cost Ratio = ($40k * 5yr) / $100k = 2.0 or 2:1

INITIATING PROCESS GROUP

4.1 Develop Project Charter ITTOs – PMBOK ® Guide Page 75
Generic categories are listed under the primary ITTOs in the chart

Make sure you understand the purpose of the project charter, which is to formally **authorize** the project or phase to begin and to begin committing **organizational resources.**

Become Better Prepared by Practicing This

Which Input is referenced in the right column?	
OPAs	Project management procedures, safety policies, and a knowledge base.
EEFs	Includes things such as the organization's work authorization system.
Agreements	Documents that define the intent of the project and are usually legal in nature.
Business Case	Describes the need for the project and determines if the investment in the project is worthwhile.

Do These Steps to Fully Prepare:

Indicate if these statements are true or false:

True or False: The project isn't a project until the charter is signed.

True or False: Writing the business case occurs outside the project boundaries.

True or False: Project management software is an EEF.

True or False: Political climate is an EEF.

True or False: If pressed to start a project before a signed charter is approved, a project manager should request the project charter gets approved prior to proceeding.

True or **False**: Lessons learned are an EEF.

13.1 Identify Stakeholders ITTOs – PMBOK ® Guide Page 507

Generic categories are listed under the primary ITTOs in the chart

Become Better Prepared by Practicing This

Power/Interest Grid:

	Keep Satisfied	**Monitor Closely**
>> HIGH Power	Engage and consult Increase or maintain level of interest Understand and satisfy their needs Keep them informed Monitor their interest	Keep actively involved in project and decisions Develop solid relationship Their cooperation is project critical
LOW Power >>>	**Monitor (Minimal effort required)** Communicate generally to keep updated Include them in status reporting	**Keep Informed** Consult on their area of interest Sell the initiative to the group
	LOW INTEREST	**HIGH INTEREST**

Practice: Perform These Steps to Fully Prepare

Salience Model

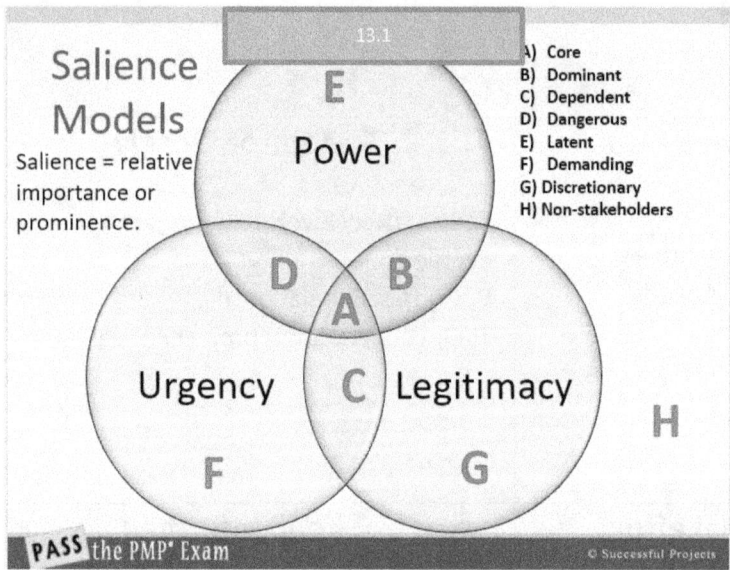

Salience Model Stakeholder Types:

I. **Core**: These are critical project stakeholders. As a Project Manager, you need to provide focused attention to these stakeholders.
J. **Dominant**: These project stakeholders have power and legitimacy, but do not have urgency. You should focus on their expectations, but there is not a lot of urgency.
K. **Dependent**: These project stakeholders have no real power on the project. However, they need to be managed because they can quite easily choose to align themselves with other project stakeholders and hence influence your project.
L. **Dangerous**: What an appropriately named classification. These stakeholders have power and urgency, but no legitimacy. Imagine a very senior person trying to force her views on the outcome of your project, without really being a part of it! A Project Manager needs to keep such stakeholders appropriately engaged or satisfied.
M. **Latent**: Possibly the best category project stakeholders. These stakeholders only get into the project if there is something that has gone horribly wrong with it. Over-communication of micro-level details with them is not a great thing to do.
N. **Demanding**: Such stakeholders are people that always seem to think that their work needs your immediate attention. If you spend too much time and effort on these stakeholders, you won't gain too much project mileage. There are other more important people to work with.
O. **Discretionary**: Another wonderful classification of project stakeholder. Give them regular status updates and they'll be happy.
P. **Non-stakeholders**: These people are not stakeholders in the project. Investing time and effort on such people will not help you shape the outcome of your project in any manner.

Section 6: Planning Processes – Integration and Scope

Planning Process Group – Integration Management and Scope Management

4.2 Develop Project Management Plan ITTOs – PMBOK ® Guide Page 82
Generic categories are listed under the primary ITTOs in the chart.

Become Better Prepared by Practicing This

What Goes in the Project Management Plan?

Check your answers against Table 4-1 on page 89 of the *PMBOK® Guide.*

Do These Steps to Fully Prepare

Understanding Baseline Plans

Complete this sentence.

Once the project management plan is baselined, it may only be changed when it has gone through 4.6 Perform Integrated Change Control process.

5.1 Plan Scope Management ITTOs – PMBOK ® Guide Page 134
Generic categories are listed under the primary ITTOs in the chart.

Become Better Prepared by Practicing This

Two outputs from Plan Scope Management

1) The **scope management plan** is a component of the project management plan that describes how the scope will be defined, developed, monitored, controlled, and validated.
2) The **requirements management plan** is a component of the project management plan that describes how the requirements will be analyzed, documented, and managed.

Do These Steps to Fully Prepare

Do you fully understand what configuration management and a configuration management system is?

Configuration management is essentially a version control system for the product of the project. It is a component of the project management plan that describes how to identify and account for project artifacts under configuration control, and how to record and report changes to them.

5.2 Collect Requirements – PMBOK ® Guide Page 138

Generic categories are listed under the primary ITTOs in the chart.

Data Gathering Techniques

See page 142-143 of the PMBOK for descriptions of each technique.

- Brainstorming
- Focus groups
- Interviews
- Questionnaires and surveys
- Benchmarking

Become Better Prepared by Practicing This

Problems with Scope prior to requirements:

- You may well miss vital requirements. You may inadvertently narrow your scope or you may over broadly define the scope. You may not get the authorization to develop the system that you really need.

Issues - WBS prior to requirements:

- WBS must contain 100% of the project work. That means we must consider all pieces of work to be done under the scope of a particular project. So, without the requirements, we would not be able to define all of the work that will be needed for the project.

Problems with Requirements prior to scope management plan:

- The scope management plan sets the authorized parameters for the project. Without those parameters, you may start developing requirements for an unauthorized project.

Validate that you understand the difference between these methods for making decisions.

- **Unanimity**: Every group member agrees to the same decision.
-
    Majority: More than half of the group members should agree on the same result.

- **Plurality**: 50% of a group is not required in this case. Instead the decision is taken by the biggest block of people that come to the same result within the project group.

- **Autocratic**: There is one person who has the authority to make the decision for the all group members.

Do These Steps to Fully Prepare

Traceability Matrix - Example

REQUIREMENTS TRACEABILITY MATRIX					
Project Name: Online Flight Booking Application					
Business Requirements Document BRD		Functional Requirements Document FSD			Test Case Document
Business Requirement ID#	Business Requirement / Business Use case	Functional Requirement ID#	Functional Requirement / Use Case	Priority	Test Case ID#
BR_1	Reservation Module	FR_1	One Way Ticket booking	High	TC#001 TC#002
		FR_2	Round Way Ticket		TC#003 TC#004
		FR_3	Multicity Ticket booking	High	TC#005 TC#006
BR_2	Payment Module	FR_4	By Credit Card	High	TC#007 TC#008
		FR_5	By Debit Card	High	TC#009
		FR_6	By Reward Points	Medium	TC#010 TC#011

5.3 Define Scope – ITTOs PMBOK ® Guide Page 150

Generic categories are listed under the primary ITTOs in the chart.

Become Better Prepared by Practicing This

What is the difference between a Project Charter and a Scope Statement?

They both itemize the scope of the project at some level. The Charter is a high-level document that authorizes the project and is prepared by the Sponsor. The Scope Statement is prepared by the project team and tries to encompass the full scope of the project in a few paragraphs.

Do These Steps to Fully Prepare

Note examples of constraints on your projects:
- Schedule and budget constraints
- Laws and regulations
- Organization structure
- Resource availability
- Quality constraints
- Technology constraints
- Contractual constraints

Note examples of assumptions on your projects:
- That staff from other areas will be available at the defined times
- The newest release of MS Office will be installed on all office computers
- That office staff will be able to be relocated to the new office before a certain date
- That state regulations will remain stable during the project development

5.4 Create WBS ITTOs – PMBOK ® Guide Page 156
Generic categories are listed under the primary ITTOs in the chart

What are the benefits associated with developing and using a Work Breakdown Structure?

- Organizes work to be done.
- It is inclusive. If it is not on the WBS, it is not in the project.
- It subdivides the deliverables and it creates logical groupings.
- The WBS is the basis for schedule and cost estimates.
- It is also the basis for assigning responsibilities and for measurement & control.
- The WBS helps improve our plan because it minimizes omitted work and it helps us see if there are duplicated tasks.
- It helps control development of the plan for the entire project.
- It provides an increased visibility of scope to all stakeholders.
- It also provides input to other knowledge areas outside of scope. It is very key part of the Project Management Plan.

Scope baseline includes:

The scope baseline is a part of the project management plan and acts as a reference point throughout the project's life. It has several components including: the project scope document, the WBS itself and the WBS dictionary.

<u>Become Better Prepared by Practicing This</u>

Code of Accounts and Control Account

- Code of Accounts: A numbering system used to uniquely identify each component of the work breakdown structure.

- Control Account: are placed at selected management points in the WBS. Each Control Account is defined with a unique code or an accounting number which can be used to link to the performing account system.

Section 7: Planning Processes – Schedule

PLANNING PROCESS GROUP - SCHEDULE

6.1 Plan Schedule Management ITTOs – PMBOK ® Guide Page 179
Generic categories are listed under the primary ITTOs in the chart

Become Better Prepared by Practicing This

Agile/Adaptive Environments: PMBOK p. 178

- The Role of the project manager does not change but the project manager needs to be familiar with the associated tools and techniques used in an agile environment.

Levels of Accuracy

- Specifies the acceptable range used in determining realistic activity duration and may include an amount for contingencies.
- Provides guidelines regarding accuracy levels expected in time estimates.
- Accuracy is an assessment of correctness.
- The project management team should determine the appropriate levels of accuracy.

6.2 Define Activities ITTOs – PMBOK ® Guide Page 183
Generic categories are listed under the primary ITTOs in the chart

Become Better Prepared by Practicing This

Work Package is the work defined at the lowest level of the work breakdown structure for which cost and duration can be estimated and managed.

It...

- is the smallest level of a deliverable.
- is the lowest component of a WBS.
- cannot be broken down further. It cannot be decomposed into a smaller level deliverable.
- provides some tangible value to the project stakeholder(s).

An **Activity** is a distinct, scheduled portion of work performed during the course of a project.
A series of activities results in, or creates, a Work Package.

Rolling Wave - Summarized as a phased, 'plan a little, do a little' approach. Detailed planning is done for activities in near term and high-level planning for activities to be performed far away in the future. As the project progresses, and requirements become clearer, more detailed planning is done for the work packages at lower levels of the WBS.

WBS Decomposition - A WBS can be oriented around deliverables or can break down project phases and milestones for a process-centered approach. The decomposition will be at the right level when it will be able to name the deliverables required or the milestones that must be reached.

Activities vs Milestones - Activities must be performed to reach the project goals and objectives. These activities are usually as small as item to be completed in hours or in days. Such as: Define project benefits.

Milestones are not an activity and generally not assigned to any resource. But, they reflect a significant point in the project such as: Delivery of cost benefit analysis to the sponsor.

Level of Effort (LOE) - Level of Effort is supportive work that does not produce definitive output but is measured with (passage of) time. Level of Effort activities support an activity or the whole project. Since a LOE activity is not itself a work item directly associated with accomplishing the final project product, service or result, but rather one that supports such work, its duration is based on the duration of the discrete work activity it is supporting. Wikipedia uses the following example: oiling machinery will start when manufacturing starts and finish when it finishes.

Do These Steps to Fully Prepare

Activity Attributes

During the initial stages of the project, they include the UNIQUE ACTIVITY IDENTIFIER (ID), WBS ID, *and* ACTIVITY LABEL OR NAME. *When completed, they may include* ACTIVITY DESCRIPTIONS, PREDECESSOR ACTIVITIES, SUCCESSOR ACTIVITIES, LOGICAL RELATIONSHIPS, LEADS AND LAGS *(Section 6.3.2.3),* RESOURCE REQUIREMENTS, IMPOSED DATES, CONSTRAINTS, *and* ASSUMPTIONS. *Activity attributes can be used to identify the* PLACE *where the work has to be performed, the project* CALENDAR *the* ACTIVITY *is assigned to, and* TYPE OF EFFORT *involved.*

6.3 Sequence Activities ITTOs – PMBOK ® Guide Page 187
Generic categories are listed under the primary ITTOs in the chart.

Become Better Prepared by Practicing This

The Four dependency types:

- Mandatory (hard logic), are those that are legally or contractually required i.e. bank closing on a home must occur prior to moving into the home.
- Discretionary (Soft logic), There could be more than one way to define the sequence between 2 activities, however, there may be a preference of one sequence over the other sequences. The new home owner may choose to paint all the rooms in the home prior to moving into the home.
- External dependencies (dependencies that are outside of the actual project, the team has no control over, and can affect the project critical path). The non-project activities are done by people who are external to the Project Team. The electric company must provide the electric hook-up prior to the power being available to the construction team.

- Internal dependencies (generally inside the teams control), i.e. the kitchen cabinets must be installed prior to the staining of the cabinets.

Define these terms in your own words:

Hammock Activity: A Hammock Activity is a schedule or project planning term for grouping smaller subtasks that hang between two dates.

Hanger: Is an unintentional break in the network diagram because we have omitted something.

<u>Become Better Prepared by Practicing This</u>

Is this lead or lag?

1. Lag
2. Lag
3. Lag
4. Lead
5. Lead

6.4 Estimate Activity Durations ITTOs – PMBOK ® Guide Page 195

Generic categories are listed under the primary ITTOs in the chart.

Define Best Practices

According to Wikipedia: A **best practice** is a method or technique that has been generally accepted as superior to any alternatives because it produces results that are superior to those achieved by other means or because it has become a standard way of doing things, e.g., a standard way of complying with legal or ethical requirements.

Top-Down Estimates

1. Analogous - estimates use previous similar projects as a basis for estimating.

2. Parametric - estimates use a mathematical model such as total square feet multiplied by the cost per square foot.

<u>Become Better Prepared by Practicing This</u>

1 sigma = __68%____ confidence level. This is within + or minus one standard deviation from the mean.

2 sigma = __95%____ confidence level. This is within + or minus two standard deviations from the mean.

3 sigma = _99.7%__ confidence level. This is within + or minus three standard deviations from the mean.

6 sigma = 99.99%__ confidence level. This is within + or minus six standard deviations from the mean.

Do These Steps to Fully Prepare

Weighted PERT Practice

Pert Estimate = (Optimistic + (4 X Most Likely) + Pessimistic)/6

See calculator at http://magnaqm.com/project-management-tools/pert-calculator/

Box 1 (2, 4, 6) = 4

Box 2 (10, 20, 30) = 20

Box 3 (25, 50, 83) = 51.33

List approaches to Group Decision Making

- Brainstorming
- Nominal Group Technique
- Delphi
- Polling

What is Reserve analysis?

There are two types of reserves that may be factored into the time estimates, they are contingency reserves and management reserves.

Contingency reserves are sometimes called time reserves or buffers. Contingency reserves are directed towards specific deliverables or activities.

Management reserves are based on the overall project duration and they are reserved for unforeseen work that is within the scope of the project - but that we just can't clearly identify.

Practice using the probability associated with Normal Distribution Curve

Practice this with the question below (without looking at the answer if you can).

Question:

The standard deviation is (P-O)/6. 20/6 is giving us 3.333. We are looking for a 95% probability, so from our mean of 20 we subtract 2 3.333 – which is 6.666.*

And 20 – 6.67 (rounded) is 13.4.

And 20 + 6.66 is 26.66. So, C is the correct answer.

6.5 Develop Schedule ITTOs – PMBOK ® Guide Page 205

Generic categories are listed under the primary ITTOs in the chart.

Note examples of these factors in your projects:

Resource Calendar:

The resource calendar refers to the specific calendar that lists all of the working days as well as all of the nonworking days that the project management team and or the project management team leader need to utilize in order to determine the specific dates on which a specific <u>resource</u> of element is being utilized or engaged, versus the dates on which they may in fact be inactive.

Constraints:

Constraints are anything that restricts or dictates the actions of the project team. The triple constraints—scope, schedule, budget, as well as resources, and quality - are the major ones.

<u>Become Better Prepared by Practicing This</u>

Network Diagramming

Answers

Very Easy

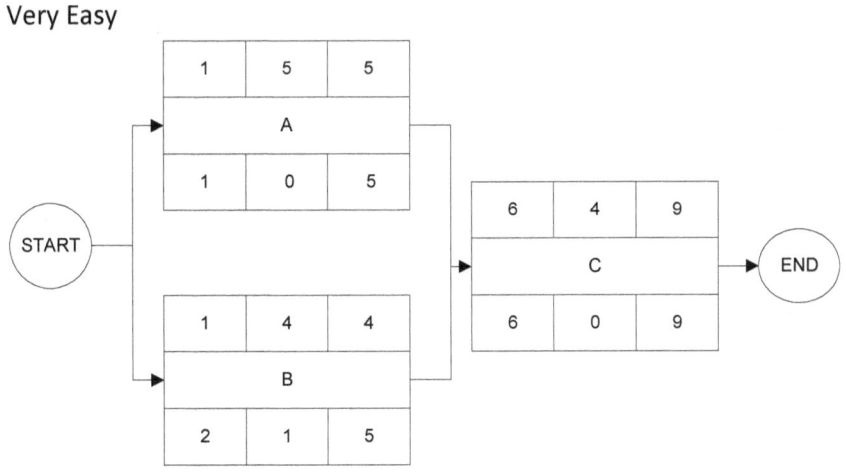

Easy

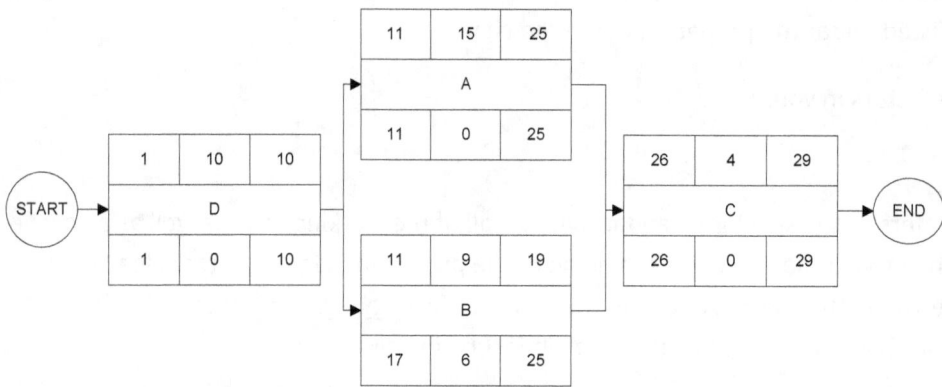

Moderate

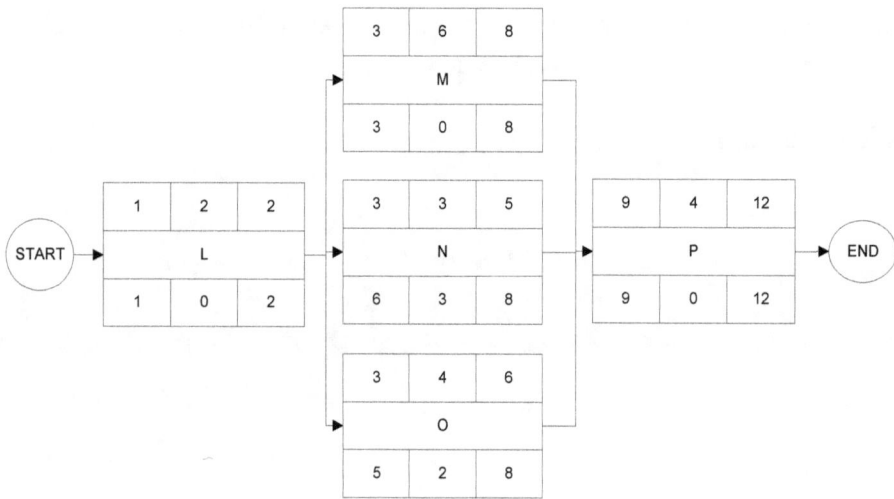

Difficult

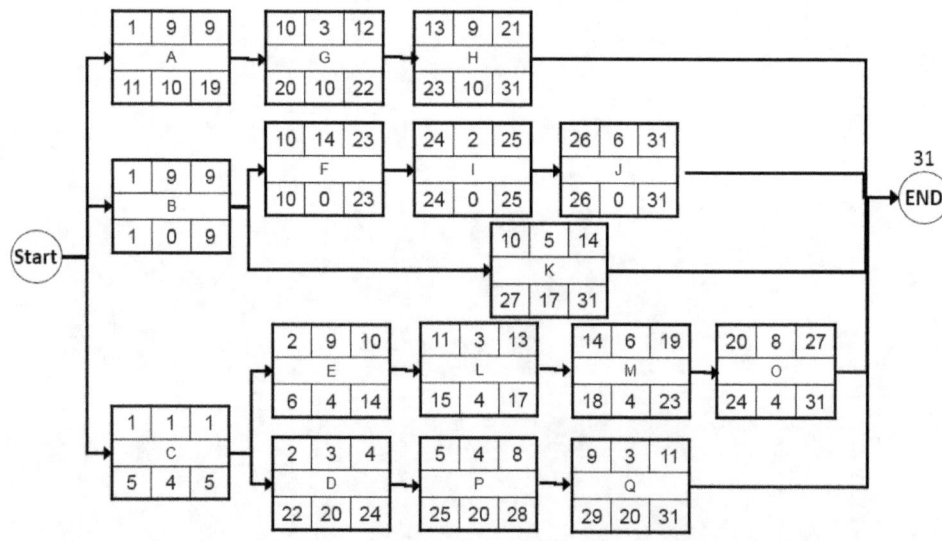

Travel Network Diagram

Answers will differ based on flight departure time selected.

Do These Steps to Fully Prepare

Network Diagrams to Calculate from Tables:

On Project A, the critical path was ACFHI. The duration was 21. Activity B's float is impacted due to the start-to-start relationship with D. There is potential that B could start just enough to start D, and then it could utilize its float before finishing.

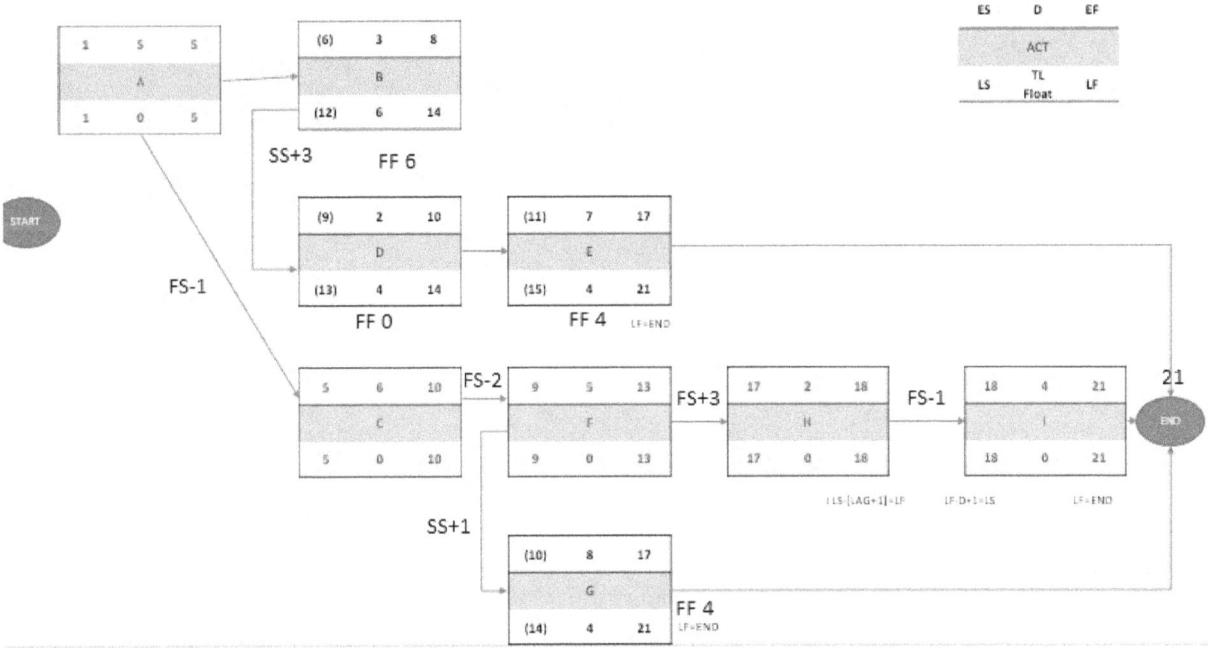

On Project B, the critical path was CFG and it had a duration of 32.

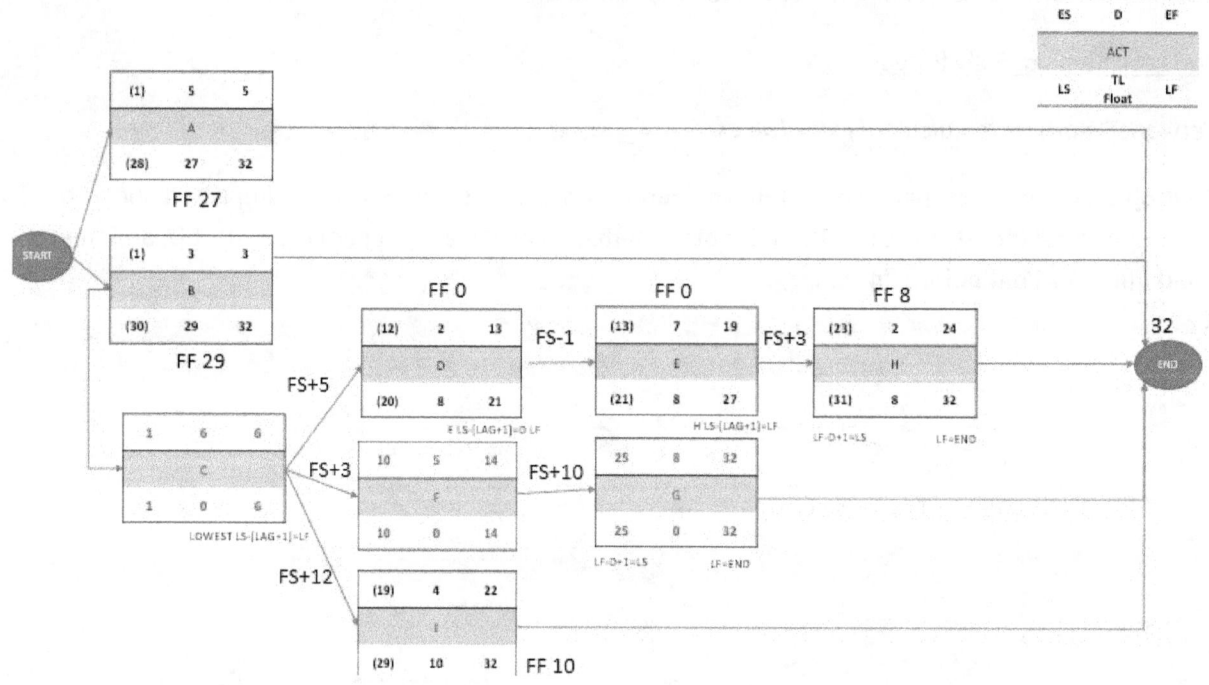

On project C, the critical path is ABCDE with a duration of 65. You will note that the S-S relationship of E to D again causes an issue with the late start of D – forcing it to be 50 (although the late finish may be 65 – therefore making the float hard to define and prone to allowing the activity to start and stop). The late start of E is 49 and its late finish is 65. Remember that the -1 indicates a lead between the S-S of D to E. It may seem strange that the dependency relationship of D to E has a lead - when it might have been done as an E to D dependency with a lag of 1 instead. But the dependency relationship given in a problem must be assumed to be correctly defined. It may help to think of a track relay race where the person grabbing the baton (E) starts running to gain speed before D can pass the baton.

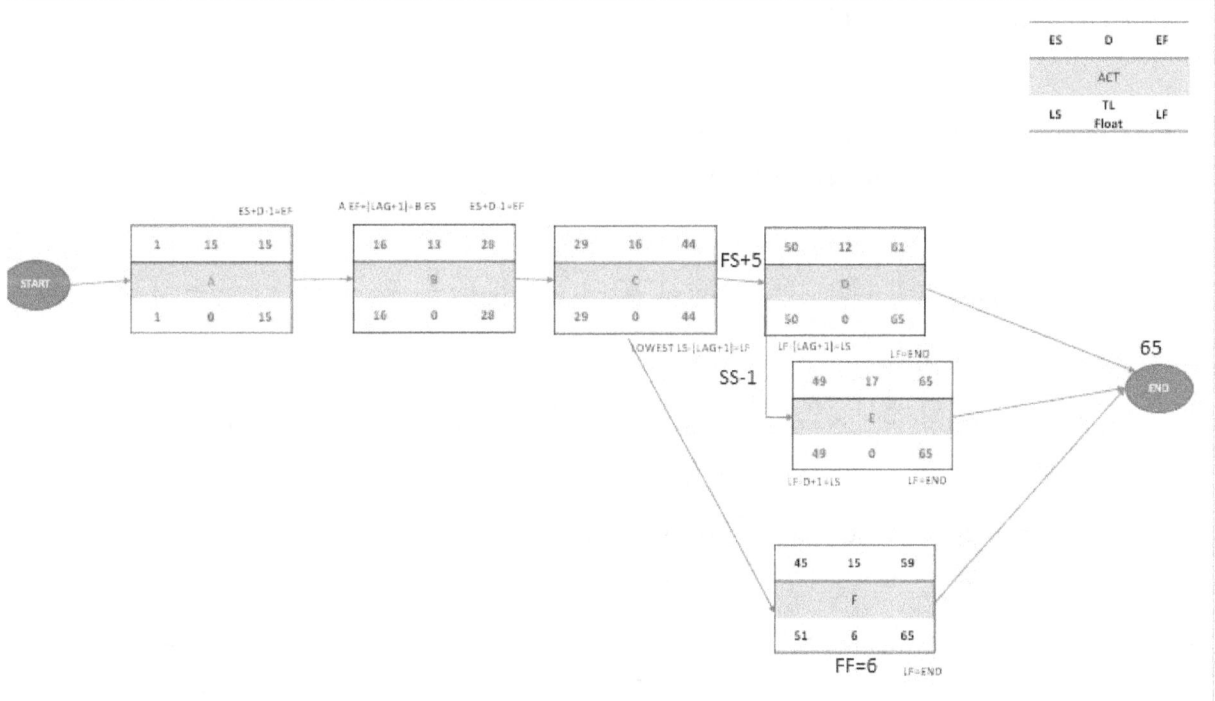

Define These Terms

Resource optimization is the set of processes and methods to match the available **resources** (human, machinery, financial) with the needs of the organization in order to achieve established goals.

Resource Leveling: Resource Leveling is a resource optimization technique in which the Project Manager adjusts the start dates and finish dates of different activities in order to balance the demand for resources vs available supply.

Define these Schedule Compression terms in your own words:

Crashing is a schedule compression technique where you add extra resources to the project to compress the schedule. In crashing, you review the critical path and see which activities can be completed by adding extra resources.

In **fast tracking**, you review the critical path to find out which sequential activities can be performed parallel or partially parallel to each other. Fast tracking helps you reduce the duration of the schedule within limits. If you continue to fast track after this limit, it may increase the risk beyond acceptable levels and lead to possible rework or future delays.

Section 8: Planning Processes - Cost

PLANNING PROCESS GROUP – COST

7.1 Plan Cost Management PMBOK ® Guide Page 235
Generic categories are listed under the primary ITTOs in the chart.

7.2 Estimate Costs - PMBOK ® Guide Page 240
Generic categories are listed under the primary ITTOs in the chart.

Get Better by Practicing This

These are estimating tools and techniques that are used to produce cost estimates and a cost budget. *Define each term in your own words:*

Analogous Estimations are based on the experience of the team or the history of the project. The estimates are made based on the time or cost taken by similar projects.

Parametric Estimation, compared to analogous estimation, stands to be more accurate. Parametric estimates are based on parameters that define the complexity, risk and costs of a program, project, service, process or activity. Parametric uses an algorithm or standard to produce a higher level of accuracy (such as price per square foot).

Bottom-up Estimating - A work breakdown structure divides project deliverables into a series of work packages (each work package comprised of a series of tasks). The project team estimates the cost of completing each task, and eventually creates a cost estimate for the entire project by totaling the costs of all its constituent tasks and work packages.

Three-point estimating - Estimates may be improved by considering risk in order to create three estimates: the most-likely (cM), optimistic (cO), and pessimistic (cP) cost estimate. These three estimates are combined in either the triangular or beta distribution.

Alternative Analysis - Compares multiple potential solutions in the context of a specific problem, design goal, or policy objective. It is intended to inform decision-making in situations with many possible courses of action, a wide range of variables to consider, or significant degrees of uncertainty.

Reserve Analysis - There's really two parts that you need to know about reserves, and those are contingency and management reserves.

Contingency Reserves are for known-unknowns. These are the negative risks that you plan for on a project.

Management Reserves are for unknowns-unknowns. These are the risks you don't plan for — and management gets to decide if and when these reserves are released.

Cost of Quality (COQ) can be defined as costs associated with quality-related efforts and deficiencies. These include assuring, preventing, detecting, and remediating product issues related to quality. Quality involves creating, maintaining, upgrading and delivering a product while having some standards that meets or exceeds the expectations of the customers. There are two classifications of cost: cost of conformance and cost of non-conformance.

Vendor Bid Analysis - This procurement stage is when the project team collects all information together to compare various bids, along with the technical and commercial details of each.

Project Management Information System (PMIS) - An information system consisting of the tools and techniques used to gather, integrate, and disseminate the outputs of project management processes.

Decision-Making Techniques include: Voting - Unanimity (including the Delphi Technique), Majority, Plurality, and Dictatorship/Autocratic, and Multi-criteria Decision Analysis.

7.3 Determine Budget – PMBOK ® Guide Page 248
Generic categories are listed under the primary ITTOs in the chart.

<u>Get Better by Practicing This</u>

Define Reserve Analysis and Management Reserves

There are two types of reserves that may be factored into the time estimates. They are contingency reserves and management reserves.
- Contingency reserves are sometimes called time reserves or buffers. Contingency reserves are directed towards specific deliverables or activities.
- Management reserves are based on the overall project duration and they are reserved for unforeseen work that is within the scope of the project - but that we just can't clearly identify.

Do These Steps to Fully Prepare

What is a Funding Limit Reconciliation?

It is the process of comparing planned expenditure of project funds against any limits on the commitment of funds for the project in order to identify any variances between the funding limits and the planned expenditures. This becomes necessary if the project schedule shows a certain amount of work being done, but the project scope statement has a constraint on the availability of funds for a particular time period or periods.

Section 9: Planning Processes (continued)

PLANNING PROCESS GROUP – QUALITY, RESOURCE, COMMUNICATIONS, RISK, PROCUREMENT, and STAKEHOLDER

8.1 Plan Quality Management – PMBOK ® Guide Page 277
Generic categories are listed under the primary ITTOs in the chart.

Remember the Quality Gurus

Draw a line to connect the Quality Guru with their associated Quality Theory

                        Plan ~ Do ~ Check ~ Act cycle – W. Deming

                        Zero Defects – P. Crosby

                        Taguchi methodology involving prototyping – G. Taguchi

                        Responsibility for quality is on management. Very into the Pareto Principle – J.M. Juran

Cost of Quality

Note examples of each type shown above.

Internal Failure Costs – Corrections to defects found before delivery to customer - rework

External Failure Costs - warranties, recalls, repairs

Appraisal Costs - The inspection of materials delivered from suppliers, the inspection of work-in-process materials and of finished goods.

Prevention Costs - Improvement of manufacturing processes, workers training, quality engineering.

Become Better Prepared by Practicing This

Do you remember these values? Sigma values practice

- 1   Sigma = 68.26%
- 2   Sigma = 95.46%
- 3   Sigma = 99.73%
- 6   Sigma = 99.99% (3.4 Defects per million)

Do These Steps to Fully Prepare

Draw a sketch to remind yourself how each of the 7 different tools (which are visual) look:

You can find examples of the diagrams at http://www.whatissixsigma.net/7-qc-tools/

9.1 Plan Resource Management – PMBOK ® Guide Page 312

Generic categories are listed under the primary ITTOs in the chart.

Organizational Structures are defined as Functional, Matrix, Virtual and Project Oriented (Refer to Table 2-1 in PMBOK Guide page 47). Virtual organizations are relatively new. You may find the following online article of interest. https://www.pmi.org/learning/library/virtual-project-management-office-electronic-7037. Remember that in the functional structure the project manager has the least authority and, in the Project Oriented structure the project manager has the greatest authority. In the Balanced Matrix the project manager and Functional Managers have equal levels of authority which may result in some conflicts created by the "two boss syndrome."

Management Theories

Define these types of managers in your own words. Can you think of examples from the movies?

Theory X: According to this theory, managers assume that your employees are inherently lazy and will avoid work if they can. Hence it is believed that your people need to be closely supervised and comprehensive systems of control need to put in place. As an example, how about Gary Cole as the office boss Bill Lumbergh in the 1999 film Office Space?

Theory Y: managers believe that your employees enjoy their work and there is a chance for greater productivity by giving your people the freedom to perform to the best of their abilities, without being bogged down by rules. A Theory Y manager believes that, given the right conditions, most people will want to do well at work and that there is a pool of unused creativity in the workforce. They also believe that the satisfaction of doing a good job is a strong motivation in itself. As an example, how about William Shatner, Captain Kirk as the boss of the Starship Enterprise on Star Trek? While his time at the helm wasn't always smooth Kirk could always be counted on as an innovative and quick-thinking leader.

Theory Z: Theory Z is a mix of practices which ensure, a healthy blend of systems and the freedom to perform at the work place, is likely to motivate the employees more. This mix of practices usually requires technology built into your HR systems to be realized completely. Theory Z builds on Theory Y of motivation in the work place. Here the focus is on ensuring that your company has a strong set of values and offers a long-range approach to training and development and a highly participatory style of management. For Ouchi, Theory Z focused on increasing employee loyalty to the company by providing a job for life with a strong focus on the well-being of the employee, both on and off the job. According to Ouchi, Theory Z management tends to promote stable employment, high productivity, and high employee morale and satisfaction. As an example here, how about Miranda Bailey from Grey's Anatomy? She is known as "The Nazi" because of her tough, demanding personality and unforgiving blunt attitude. But, she is also known to have a softer, more understanding and supportive side and her staff is loyal to her.

9.2 Estimate Activity Resources – PMBOK ® Guide Page 321

Generic categories are listed under the primary ITTOs in the chart.

<u>Get Better by Practicing This</u>

Important Inputs

Resource Calendar - The resource calendar refers to the specific calendar that lists working days and nonworking days to determine specific dates on which a resource is being utilized or engaged, versus the dates they are inactive.

Risk Register – A prioritized list of risks with details about probability and impact, and risk responses. The risk register includes all information about each identified risk, such as the nature of that risk, level of risk, who owns it and what mitigation measures are in place to respond to it.

Important Tools and Techniques

Bottom–up Resource Estimating - Bottom up estimating requires the use of the WBS and will produce "definitive" estimates by aggregating the information from the lowest levels of the WBS (the work packages) to the top level. Bottom up estimating is more reliable but will require more time and effort. A bottom-up estimate will generally produce an estimate that is within + or – 10% of the actual result. The bottom-up estimate requires the greatest effort, in terms of time and resources, to produce.

Major Output

Resource Breakdown Structure - According to Wikipedia - In project management, the resource breakdown structure (RBS) is a hierarchical list of resources related by function and resource type that is used to facilitate planning and controlling of project work. The Resource Breakdown Structure includes, at a minimum, the personnel resources needed for successful completion of a project, and preferably contains all resources on which project funds will be spent, including personnel, tools, machinery, materials, equipment and fees and licenses.

10.1 Plan Communications Management – PMBOK ® Guide Page 366

Generic categories are listed under the primary ITTOs in the chart.

5 C's of Communication

- Correct grammar
- Concise expression
- Clear purpose and expression
- Coherent logical flow of ideas
- Controlling flow of words and ideas

Become Better Prepared by Practicing This

Communications Methods - Note an example of when each type is most appropriate:

Interactive Communication: In this method two or more people interact with each other. Meetings, conference calls, video conferences are examples of Interactive communication.

Push Communication: Unlike interactive communication, this method involves sending the information to the recipient with no expectation of receiving feedback. This is one-way streaming of information. Status reports, mass-mailers, project updates sent to a large population are examples of push communication.

Pull Communication: In this method, the sender places the information at a central location (like a SharePoint or a share drive) and it's the recipients responsibility to retrieve the details from that location.

Communications Plan: Use the space below to outline some of the key information that could be included in this subsidiary plan.

Refer to Page 377 *PMBOK® Guide* for a list of potential information to include.

Do These Steps to Fully Prepare

Channels of communication

The total number of potential communication channels is n (n – 1) /2, where n represents the number of stakeholders.

5 people =10 channels

6 people =15 channels

9 people =36 channels

12 people =66 channels

11.1 Plan Risk Management - PMBOK ® Guide Page 401
Generic categories are listed under the primary ITTOs in the chart.

Define Risks and Issues – what are the differences?

- Risk is an event or condition that, if it occurs, has a positive <u>or</u> negative effect on a project objective or deliverable.
- Issues are known occurring problems, or currently active situations that, if left unresolved may result in a risk event.

Define the relationship between overall project risk and project timing:

One consistent guideline is that risk management planning should always be started early in the overall project planning process. That helps you take preventative action in whatever you may be faced with, such as planning in advance to have a parachute if you may be falling off a cliff.

Total project risk decreases as we move toward project completion, but the amount at stake increases toward the end of the project life cycle.

11.2 Identify Risks - PMBOK ® Guide Page 409
Generic categories are listed under the primary ITTOs in the chart.

Risks and Characteristics:

Risk Breakdown Structure: Risks are seldom found alone. They usually travel in packs! Risk breakdown structures are ways of organizing risks into sensible groupings. As you are collecting risks, it often makes sense to assign categories of risks to the same owner.

Risk Register: Most of today's project managers track their risks in a spreadsheet risk register. Many get the base template from their organizational process assets. In some cases, the categories or common risks are pre-populated.

Become Better Prepared by Practicing This

Information gathering processes

Delphi: An information gathering technique used as a way to reach consensus of experts on a subject. Experts on the subject participate in this technique anonymously.

Brainstorming: This technique is facilitated either free-form or a structured mass interview.

Interviewing: Talking with experienced project experts, including project team members, stakeholders, and subject matter experts and getting their help in identifying risks.

Root cause analysis: This is a very specific technique used to identify a problem, discover the underlying causes that lead to it, and develop preventive action.

SWOT Analysis: Examines the project from each of the strengths, weaknesses, opportunities, and threats perspectives.

11.3 Perform Qualitative Risk Analysis - PMBOK ® Guide Page 419
Generic categories are listed under the primary ITTOs in the chart.

11.4 Perform Quantitative Risk Analysis - PMBOK ® Guide Page 428
Generic categories are listed under the primary ITTOs in the chart.

Become Better Prepared by Practicing This

Probability Distributions – Draw a sketch Beta, Normal, Uniform, Triangular

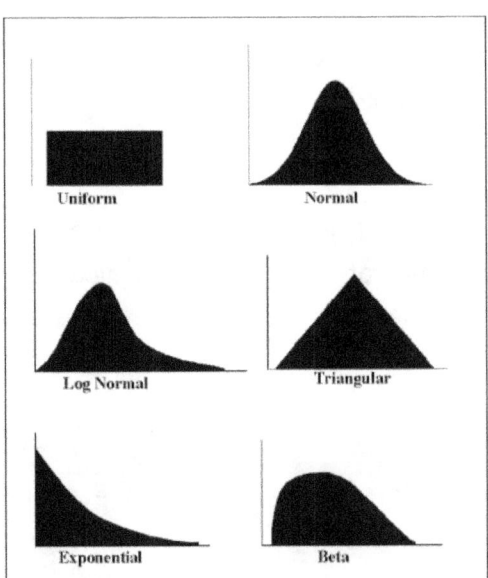

Define Sensitivity Analysis in your own words

Determines what risks have the most potential impact on a project. It analyzes the uncertainty of how much a project element affects an objective when all other uncertainties are held at their baseline values.

Do These Steps to Fully Prepare

Residual Risk examples:

- A business decides to avoid the risk of developing a new technology because the project has many risks. The residual risk is that a competitor will develop the technology instead and the business will become less competitive.

- An airline reduces the risk of an accident by improving maintenance procedures. Residual risks remain in the process including a chance of human error such as skipping steps in the procedure.

Secondary Risk examples:

Prior to travelling, you get your immunization vaccines updated to avoid any diseases.

- The secondary risk would be the vaccines themselves may cause side effects (including prolonged fatigue or headache) or even cause infection. You may need a risk response plan for this secondary risk.

Prior to the PMP exam, you may decide to forego breakfast in fear of an upset stomach.

- Secondary risk may be that you will be so hungry that you cannot concentrate. You may want to plan on taking some energy bars with you.

11.5 Plan Risk Responses - PMBOK ® Guide Page 437
Generic categories are listed under the primary ITTOs in the chart.

Define Contingent response:

A contingent response strategy is developed in advance and designed to be used only if the risk event occurs. Example: You are wrapping up a major project. As part of closing, you are going to sponsor an outdoor barbecue. You may want to identify a covered location that is nearby as an alternate location in case of rain.

Become Better Prepared by Practicing This

Risk Strategies

Positive:

- Escalate is one strategy which we can use if we identify a risk that does not affect our objectives or falls outside of the scope of the project, but that could affect some other part of the organization.
- Exploit is taking action to ensure the opportunity is realized.
- Share is allocating some, or all of the ownership of the opportunity, to a third party who is best able to capture the opportunity for the benefit of the project.
- Enhance is taking action to increase the probability or impacts of a possible opportunity.
- Accept response is acknowledging the risk and deciding not to take any action unless it occurs.

Negative:

- Escalate is one strategy which we can use if we identify a risk that does not affect our objectives or falls outside of the scope of the project, but that could affect some other part of the organization.
- Mitigate is taking actions to reduce a risk by minimizing the impact and / or the probability of the risk.
- Transfer / Insure is determining the risk should be shifted to a third party, together with the ownership of the response.
- Avoid is determining the risk should be taken out of the project.
- Accept response is acknowledging the risk and deciding not to take any action unless it occurs.

12.1 Plan Procurement Management - PMBOK ® Guide Page 466

Generic categories are listed under the primary ITTOs in the chart.

Become Better Prepared by Practicing This

Contract Types

Fixed Price - Fixed-Price contracts are good to use for products or services that a seller creates repeatedly. A fixed-price contract should only be used when the seller is confident in the process it takes to complete a product or service.

Cost-reimbursable contracts are used when the scope of work isn't well defined or is subject to change. This is type of contract is useful for research and development work.

Time and Material - An arrangement under which a contractor is paid on the basis of (1) actual cost of direct labor, usually at specified hourly rates, (2) actual cost of materials and equipment usage, and (3) agreed upon fixed add-on to cover the contractor's overheads and profit. (Read more: http://www.businessdictionary.com/definition/time-and-materials-T-M-contract.html)

Fixed price incentive fee offers an incentive if the product or service exceeds an expectation. For example, a buyer might give the seller an incentive fee if the seller completes the product early.

Cost plus incentive fee – contract that provides for an initially negotiated fee to be adjusted later by a formula based on the relationship of total allowable costs to total target costs.

Define Point of total assumption - The (PTA) is the point when the seller bears all the costs of a cost overrun - first cutting into their profit, and then, if it goes on long enough, it actually starts to cause a loss which increases the longer it continues. Any FPI contract specifies a target cost, a target profit, a target price, a ceiling price, and one or more share ratios. The PTA is the difference between the ceiling and target prices, divided by the buyer's portion of the share ratio for that price range, plus the target cost.

Practice this formula: ((Target cost – Actual Cost) * Seller's sharing ratio) + Target fee

Solution: PTA = ((2,450,000 - 2,200,000)/ 0.80) + 2,000,000 = 2,312,500.

13.2 Plan Stakeholder Engagement - PMBOK ® Guide Page 516
Generic categories are listed under the primary ITTOs in the chart.

<u>Become Better at Practicing This</u>

Stakeholder Management Plan: *Describe what the Stakeholder Engagement plan provides:*

A good stakeholder engagement plan provides a clear, actionable plan to interact with project stakeholders to support the project's interests. It often provides these things:
- Key stakeholders as well as current and desired engagement levels.
- Sometimes it shows how relationships between stakeholders overlap.
- It may integrate with the communication plan and plan the stakeholder communications requirements as well as plan how to communicate, how often to do so, and other proactive stakeholder planning measures.
- And ideally the plan would also state how to update and refine this plan over time.

<u>Do These Steps to Fully Prepare</u>

Stakeholder Engagement Matrix

Check your work against Figure 13-6 on p. 522 of the *PMBOK® Guide*.

- Unaware
- Resistant: resistant to change
- Neutral
- Supportive: supportive of change
- Leading: actively engaged in project success

Section 10: Executing Process Group

EXECUTING PROCESS GROUP

4.3 Direct and Manage Project Work - PMBOK ® Guide Page 90
Generic categories are listed under the primary ITTOs in the chart.

4.4 Manage Project Knowledge - PMBOK ® Guide Page 98
Generic categories are listed under the primary ITTOs in the chart.

Become Better by Practicing This

Fill in the blanks:

The most important part of knowledge management is creating an atmosphere of TRUST so that people are motivated to SHARE their KNOWLEDGE.

Do These Steps to Fully Prepare

Knowledge Management vs Information Management –What does the PMBOK share about the difference between these two terms? Knowledge Management is primarily concerned with capturing the explicit and tacit knowledge of your employees before they retire or leave; whereas, Information management is primarily concerned with collecting, processing and managing the data required to execute your organizations mission and thereby turning it into useful information. Refer to pages 102-103 in the PMBOK for examples of each.

8.2 Manage Quality - PMBOK ® Guide Page 288
Generic categories are listed under the primary ITTOs in the chart.

9.3 Acquire Resources - PMBOK ® Guide Page 328
Generic categories are listed under the primary ITTOs in the chart.

9.4 Develop Team - PMBOK ® Guide Page 336
Generic categories are listed under the primary ITTOs in the chart.

9.5 Manage Team- PMBOK ® Guide Page 345
Generic categories are listed under the primary ITTOs in the chart.

Become Better by Practicing This

Review the Composition of Project Teams

Dedicated project teams are most often seen in Functional organizations

Part-time project teams are very common in Project Based organizations

10.2 Manage Communications - PMBOK ® Guide Page 379
Generic categories are listed under the primary ITTOs in the chart.

Become Better Prepared by Practicing This

These are suggestions and not a complete list of alternatives:

1. **Levels of Formality**: 90% of a project managers time is spent in communication. A common reason for project failure is because of communication failure. It is important that the appropriate types of communications are planned for use during the manage communications process. Being present, visible and engaged with everyone is important, during good times as well as challenging times.
   - ACTIVE communication methods are those used to communicate in real time such as: personal meetings, telephone calls, video conferencing, webinars, group presentations
   - PASSIVE communication methods are those where the recipients can review in their own time, for example: webcasts, email, blogs, podcasts, websites, project status reports or newsletters and electronic dashboards.
   - Within a project, it is best to provide a mix of active and passive methods of communication.
2. **Writing style:** Describe active voice versus passive voice and indicate when each is appropriate. Active voice is where the subject performs the action. In passive voice the subject receives the action. Generally, people are discouraged from using the passive voice because it tends to obscure the true meaning of a sentence. Writing in the active voice usually communicates a message better than writing in the passive voice does. However, using the passive voice can help soften the message such as "Your change request has been denied" vs "We have denied your change request".
3. What are **meeting management** best practices? http://projectmanagementhacks.com/meeting-tips/
   - Only meet to create value
   - Plan the meeting in advance (send out agendas)
   - Start the meeting on time and expect all meeting participants to come prepared
   - Follow the agenda
   - Recap at the end of the meeting, go back and explicitly clarify action commitments
4. What are **presentation** best practices? https://www.skillsyouneed.com/present/presentation-tips.html
   - Show your Passion and Connect with your Audience.
   - Focus on your Audience's Needs.
   - Keep it Simple: Concentrate on your Core Message.
   - Smile and Make Eye Contact with your Audience.
   - Start Strongly.
   - Tell Stories.
5. What are **good techniques for building consensus** and overcoming obstacles in a group? Consensus decision-making is useful when dealing with a complex problem requiring the input of multiple stakeholders and when a creative solution is needed. The method enables teams to collaborate in an effective way.
   - Focus on big ideas versus details
   - Encourage brainstorming on alternatives
   - Explore with those who do not support an idea, what it would take for them to support it
   - Encourage active and empathetic listening
   - Take turns expressing opinions on an idea

6. What are Best Practices for **Active and accurate listening**?
Listening is often thought of as a "passive" form of communication. But, active listening actually takes a tremendous amount of energy and attention. It is a critical PM skill, and it can be very difficult to do. Good listening requires that you hone in on what is being communicated. Many project problems are caused due to miscommunication where one of the root causes can be poor listening.

Do These Steps to Fully Prepare

Sender/receiver communication model

Refer to: Figure 10.4 on p. 373 in the *PMBOK® Guide*

11.6 Implement Risk Responses - PMBOK ® Guide Page 449
Generic categories are listed under the primary ITTOs in the chart.

Become Better Prepared by Practicing This

Complete the Following Statement:
A common problem with Project Risk Management is that project teams spend effort, *in identifying and analyzing risks and developing risk responses* then risk responses are agreed upon and documented in, *the risk register and risk report* but *no action is taken to manage the risk*.
PMBOK ® Guide Page 450

12.2 Conduct Procurements - PMBOK ® Guide Page 482
Generic categories are listed under the primary ITTOs in the chart.

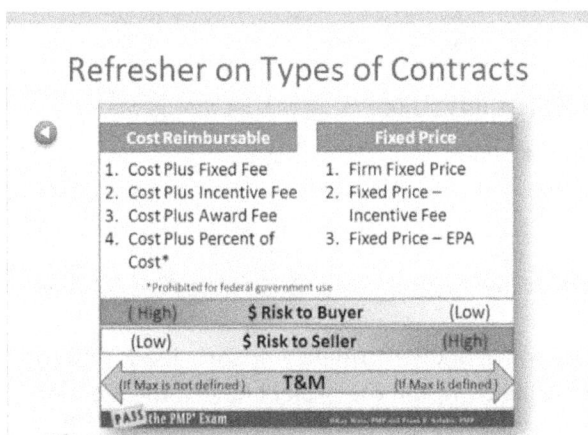

Contract Risk Answer Key

CPIF: Risk to Buyer: Medium. Risk to Seller: Medium.

CPFF: Risk to Buyer: High. Risk to Seller: Low.

T&M: Risk to Buyer: Medium. Risk to Seller: Medium.

CPPC: Risk to Buyer: Very High. Risk to Seller: Very Low.

FFP: Risk to Buyer: Very Low. Risk to Seller: Very High.

FPI: Risk to Buyer: Low. Risk to Seller: High.

13.3 Manage Stakeholder Engagement - PMBOK ® Guide Page 523
Generic categories are listed under the primary ITTOs in the chart.

Note examples of each form of communication:

Interactive communication - The communication process takes place between humans or machines in both verbal or non-verbal ways (think about automated telephone lines), using verbal and non-verbal methods (think of the difference between talking on the phone and chatting over social media).

Push communication include letters, memos, reports, emails, SMS, faxes, voice mails, blogs, press releases, etc.

Pull communications includes intranet sites, e-learning, lessons learned database, knowledge repositories, etc.

Section 11: Monitoring and Controlling Process Group

MONITORING AND CONTROLLING PROCESS GROUP

4.5 Monitor and Control Project Work - PMBOK ® Guide Page 105
Generic categories are listed under the primary ITTOs in the chart.

<u>Become Better Prepared by Practicing This</u>

Study Figure 4-11. Monitor and Control Project Work Data Flow Diagram on p. 106 of the *PMBOK Guide*.

- Pay special attention to the flow of Change Requests and Work Performance Reports feeds into the Perform Integrated Change Control process. What problems would the project have if the work on that arrow was neglected?
    - o You would run the risk of ignoring changes to your project and going over scope, schedule and budget on your project.

4.6 Perform Integrated Change Control - PMBOK ® Guide Page 113
Generic categories are listed under the primary ITTOs in the chart.

5.5 Validate Scope - PMBOK ® Guide Page 163

Generic categories are listed under the primary ITTOs in the chart.

Become Better by Practicing This

Study Figure 5-16 page 164. Validate Scope Data Flow Diagram

- What happens to unaccepted deliverables in this flow?

    Goes to 4.6 Perform integrated change control

5.6 Control Scope - PMBOK ® Guide Page 167

Generic categories are listed under the primary ITTOs in the chart.

6.6 Control Schedule - PMBOK ® Guide Page 222

Generic categories are listed under the primary ITTOs in the chart.

Become Better by Practicing This

Network Diagram

Here is the critical path and details to answer the questions below.

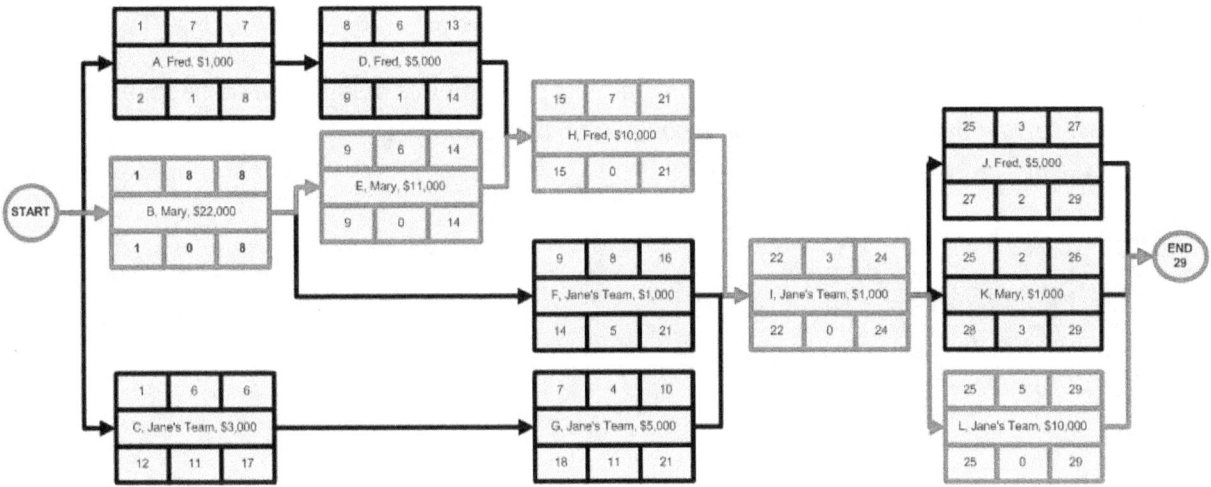

1. What activities create the project's critical path? *BEHIL*
2. What is G's slack time if C used 6 weeks of its available slack time?
   The total float time is shared on the path. Your team members need to know that. So, when we start to dip into the float time already with activity C, the 6 weeks that they used is no longer available to G. They have only 5 of the total 11 weeks left to use now on G.
3. During week 1, what activity is your greatest concern? *B as it is on the Critical Path*
4. If Jane and her Team can't do any work on this project during weeks 9 and 10, can we still work with them and achieve our schedule?

First, hopefully you identified all of the activities planned for Jane's Team in this timeframe, which is C, F, and G. Then if you look at the float time, you see they can continue on schedule despite their constraint because they have enough float to work around that scheduling conflict.

5. If you had to pick 4 milestone points in the project based on the network diagram, where would they fall?

    *Towards the beginning, the end of B is a milestone because it is a **burst point**. And it is the most expensive part of the project and it's on the critical path. The end of D/E may be a milestone because it is **a sink point** on the critical path. "I" could be a milestone either at its start or at its finish. But it's a small activity both in time and cost, so you wouldn't give it two milestone markers. Convention would tend to wrap it with the work before it, and put the milestone at the end of I. But it could go either place.*

6. Assume you are the project manager and you want to take a 2-week vacation sometime during the project. When is the best time for you to be out on vacation? Does the network diagram or Gantt chart do a better job of helping you make this decision?

    Gantt charts is a Stacked Bar Chart to represent Project Schedule in Graphical Representation. It does a good job of focusing on the schedule dates. The Networks diagram is Flow Chart representation of sequential workflow of the Project Tasks. The Gantt chart would be a better option to see the best time to take vacation. I would recommend the PM should try to take their vacation between weeks 21 ½ - 23 1/2, because nothing is starting or ending then – even if float time is used. The least amount of work is occurring, with only one activity in process.

7. Create a line chart of the cumulative planned project expenditures assuming work happens as soon as possible, and that billing is done upon completion of the activities.

    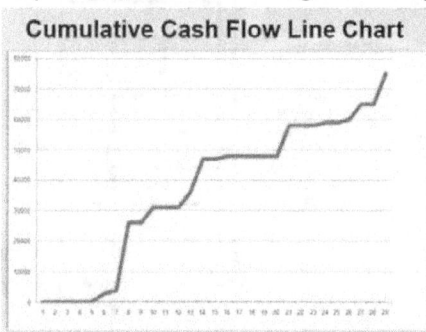

8. Compare and contrast the usefulness of the network diagram, Gantt chart, and line chart of expenditures.

    A Line chart is good for showing trends such as expenditures over time, the Gantt chart shows the scheduled activities over time, and the network diagram shows the workflow.

9. If the customer wants the project schedule shortened, what is the best activity to focus on shortening (crashing)? The second and third best? Remember that it only pays to crash the work that is on the critical path because the other work has float/slack time available.

    The first *criteria are that it has to be on the critical path. And you want to put the effort into shortening something that is not going to immediately bump the critical path off to another activity which is why you wouldn't select B or E (LOOK AT THE DURATION OF A,B,C ALL ARE VERY CLOSE*

6,7,8). Then as you look at the remaining tasks, you try to find work that can be shortened quite a bit, but where it isn't a huge percentage of the duration– so look at the longer activities. **H is the best answer because it has 7 weeks to work with, and you can shorten it by 5 weeks without altering the critical path** *(and effecting more work). we'd probably crash "I" by 2 weeks before we moved to B and L.*

10. Assuming the crash table information in the table that follows to be correct, what are the best crash priorities based purely on cost? *I followed by B and L.*

Do These Steps to Fully Prepare

Answer: The priority items for crashing are as shown below:

Task	Current Duration	Current Cost	Compressed Duration	Compressed Cost	Weekly cost to compress (crash cost)	
A	7	$1,000	3	$5,000		
B	8	$22,000	4	$30,000	$2,000	#3
C	6	$3,000	5	$4,000		
D	6	$5,000	6	$5,000		
E	6	$11,000	4	$17,000	$3,000	#4
F	8	$1,000	7	$2,000		
G	4	$5,000	2	$8,000		
H	7	$10,000	3	$25,000	$3,750	#5
I	3	$1,000	2	$2,000	$1,000	#1
J	3	$5,000	2	$6,000		
K	2	$1,000	1	$1,500		
L	5	$10,000	2	$16,000	$2,000	#2

7.4 Control Costs – PMBOK ® Guide Page 257

Generic categories are listed under the primary ITTOs in the chart.

Earned Value Drill

BCWP (EV)	BCWS (PV)	ACWP (AC)	SITUATION			
			AHEAD OF SCHEDULE	BEHIND SCHEDULE	COST UNDERRUN	COST OVERRUN
7000	9000	7000		-2000	0	0
7000	6000	5000	1000		2000	
3000	3000	6000	0	0		-3000
5000	7000	6000		-2000		-1000
7000	8000	7000		-1000	0	0
9000	6000	8000	3000		1000	
4000	3000	5000	1000			-1000
6000	7000	5000		-1000	1000	
2000	3000	4000		-1000		-2000
8000	6000	6000	2000		2000	
7000	9000	9000		-2000		-2000
5000	5000	8000	0	0		-3000
5000	4000	3000	1000		2000	
9000	7000	8000	2000		1000	
5000	5000	5000	0	0	0	0
8000	9000	7000		-1000	1000	
5000	4000	6000	1000			-1000
9000	7000	7000	2000		2000	
1000	2000	2000		-1000		-1000

<u>Do These Steps to Fully Prepare</u>

Write down the four simple EV formulas for SV, SPI, CV, and CPI:

    SV=EV-PV

    SPI=EV/PV

    CV=EV-AC

    CPI=EV/AC

8.3 Control Quality Costs – PMBOK ® Guide Page 298

Generic categories are listed under the primary ITTOs in the chart.

9.6 Control Resources Costs – PMBOK ® Guide Page 352
Generic categories are listed under the primary ITTOs in the chart.

Become Better Prepared by Practicing This

Discuss how the Project Management Information System can be beneficial in this process.

The PMIS should enable a project team to pinpoint the variances in terms of time, money and resources and see if they can find the reason why these variances have occurred. It should enable the team to track the status of each part of the project and assess the work that is completed and the resources being used.

10.3 Monitor Communications – PMBOK ® Guide Page 388
Generic categories are listed under the primary ITTOs in the chart.

11.7 Monitor Risks – PMBOK ® Guide Page 453
Generic categories are listed under the primary ITTOs in the chart.

12.3 Control Procurements – PMBOK ® Guide Page 492
Generic categories are listed under the primary ITTOs in the chart.

Become Better Prepared by Practicing This

Define these terms in your own words:

Contract change control system - Process by which the procurement can be modified. This is part of the overall Integrated Change Control System for the project. All contracts, like all projects, have changes. The first step to handling changes that arise on a contracted project is to analyze the impacts to the project, just as you would on a project without contracts or purchase orders. The change procedures in the contract must also be followed and all changes should be made formally. Changes are requested through the procurement process and are handled as part of the project integrated change control efforts.

Procurement performance reviews - A structured review of the seller's progress to deliver project scope and quality, within cost and on schedule, as compared to the contract. It identifies the success or failure of performance of the seller. It also looks at the progress in relation to the procurement statement of work and for non-compliance of the contract.

Inspections and audits Inspection is a QC process, you do it after the product is built. Audit is QA process, you do it while the product is being built to check if processes and procedures are being followed as they should be followed.

Performance reporting - Performance reporting is the process of collecting, organizing, and disseminating information on how the project resources are being used to complete the project objectives.

Payment systems – According to Wikipedia, "A **payment system** is any **system** used to settle financial transactions through the transfer of monetary value, and includes the institutions, instruments, people, rules, procedures, standards, and technologies that make such an exchange possible."

Claims administration - Claims are basically disagreements. They may be about scope, the impact of a change, or the interpretation of some piece of the contract. Contested changes to the procurement are referred to as claims, disputes, or appeals, and are resolved by the parties involved or through alternative dispute resolution (ADR).

Records management system - Records Management system (RMS) is the management of records for an organization throughout the records-life cycle. The activities include the systematic and efficient control of the creation, maintenance, and destruction of the records along with the business transactions associated with them. Considered a key component of operational efficiency, record management adds more value to organization's information assets.

13.4 Monitor Stakeholder Engagement – PMBOK ® Guide Page 530
Generic categories are listed under the primary ITTOs in the chart.

Do These Steps to Fully Prepare

How active is your project sponsor?

> Your project sponsor is the key link between the project management team and the organization's executive management. An effective sponsor "owns" the project and has the ultimate responsibility for seeing that the intended benefits are realized to create the value forecast in the business case.

> A good project sponsor will not interfere in the day-to-day running of the project -- that's the role of the project manager. But, the sponsor should help the project manager facilitate the necessary organizational support needed to make strategic decisions and create a successful project.

Are you making your issues log visible and are you getting adequate involvements from your sponsors in addressing the project issues?

> Issue logs can be viewed as a way to track errors in the project. The role it plays often extends further than this. Issue logs can be used to order and organize the current issues by type and severity in order to prioritize their importance in order to inform and engage your sponsor in helping to resolve issues.

Are you getting the best advice out of your subject matter experts?

> The right subject-matter expert (SME) can play a big role in the success of a project. Their knowledge can help take a team from good to great. Engage with them early and use their expertise for the benefit of your project.

Are your project team member's levels of engagement high?

> If your team mirrors the U.S. workforce, three out of 10 employees are fully engaged; five are "present" but engaged, and two are actively disengaged, according to the Gallup organization's <u>State of the American Workplace: 2010-2012 report</u>. Review: https://www.liquidplanner.com/blog/7-ways-to-get-your-team-members-more-engaged/

Section 12: Closing Process Group

CLOSING PROCESS GROUP

4.7 Close Project or Phase – PMBOK ® Guide Page 121
Generic categories are listed under the primary ITTOs in the chart.

www.ingramcontent.com/pod-product-compliance
Lightning Source LLC
Chambersburg PA
CBHW081203240426
43669CB00039B/2783